REMEMBER WHEN

MARK WILLIAMS

ISBN 978-1-961254-25-1 (softcover)
ISBN 978-1-961254-26-8 (ebook)

Printed in the United States of America.

INK START MEDIA
265 Eastchester Dr Ste 133 #102
High Point NC 27262

REMEMBER WHEN

A collection of
Fact, fiction, fancies and foibles

By

MARK L. WILLIAMS

For
David, Myra and Family

Remember Tommy

It was dark. That fit. He liked the dark. Dark was appropriate. The dimly lit room matched his mood. The soft, relaxed-tempo music was apropos. A dirge would be better, however, commercial establishments refrained from that sort of thing. Normally, they had a drink (or two) before adjourning to dinner. This night, they might have several drinks and skip dinner.

Douglas Newman: *Born in Norfolk in 1923. Actor and Presenter. Began acting when illness kept him out of national service. Though limited by health, he performed on the home front and for imperial service personnel, mostly in or near the Home Counties. He made his stage debut in 1947 as Puck in A Midsummer Night's Dream. He became a regular in BBC comedy and suspense radio programs. His first film was Scratch My Back in 1949 that opened the door for many similar roles in comedy pictures. For three years, he played foil and straight man for Tommy Dunn in his long-running television comedy/variety series. In 1967, he chaired the first episode of Remember When, the BBC radio comedy/chat show. He has chaired every show of every series since its debut. He is active in charity work and performs in films and stage productions. He is often seen on television, mostly in cameo roles.*

Remember When: *Since 1967, a BBC comedy series hosted by Douglas Newman and featuring four "contributors" who speak on randomly selected subjects. If the speaker wishes, he or she may defer to another panelist. A time limit of ninety seconds is imposed. Regulars include Tommy Dunn, producer/writer and comedy star of Completely Dunn; Clive Martin, film comedian, director and writer; Ian Crawford, former MP and columnist for The Daily Cryer newspaper; Colin Whitehouse, former owner and publisher of The Economic Monitor. Since the death of Gilbert Collingsworth in 1972, many guests were invited to participate whenever Ian Crawford was required in the House or abroad on government business.*

Assigned a subject, the selected celebrity is expected to wax nostalgic. Most of the anecdotes are completely fabricated and designed to encourage laughter. If another "contestant" objects to the storyteller's grammar, poor taste, historical inaccuracies, or deviation from the subject, he or she can be awarded the topic and the remaining time.

Contributors are awarded points by the chairman. Since each celebrity is paid the same amount for participation, and since no prizes are awarded, scoring is notorious. This, according to Newman, is "part of the show and part of the fun."

Newman made it a habit to be early. He preferred to greet each of the week's "panelists" as they arrived. They would have a drink and agree on a dinner venue. They would share snippets of personal events and happenings since their previous meeting. If there was a *Remember When* "virgin," Newman and the regulars would offer tips and advice. They took pains to make the first timer relaxed and comfortable. The object of their unrehearsed babbling was to entertain and, hopefully, generate laughter among the studio audience. Many experienced actors, singers and public figures were exceptionally nervous about their first appearance on *Remember When*. Whatever gaffs they make would be heard by millions in the UK and millions more around the world via the BBC World Service. Moreover, repeats of *Remember When* were broadcast from Singapore and Port Moresby to the Falklands and St. Helena, from Canada to Tasmania. If the sun never set on the defunct British Empire, there were precious few minutes when a rebroadcast of *Remember When* was not airing somewhere.

They had fun. Their humor and storytelling amused millions. Then, for the second time, the humor died. Tommy Dunn was "done."

Newman scolded himself. Even unexpressed, this pun crossed a line. However, he had to admit that Tommy would have grinned had he heard it. Tommy gloried in other people getting laughs at his expense.

He stepped up to the bar, hoping that the barman wouldn't recognize him. He wasn't in the mood for banal chatter or autographs. He was in mourning.

Normally, he went for umbrella cocktails (Tommy's diction). Tonight, however, Douglas Newman required something stiff.

"Scotch and plain water," he announced.

"In a tick, sir."

The middle-aged barman either didn't recognize him or sensed the moderator of *Remember When* was in stoic mode. When the drink arrived, he thanked the man genuinely.

He surveyed the room and looked for a large table. There was only one and it was occupied by a motionless woman staring into an untouched glass of white wine.

That's bloody rude, he thought. Even if expecting company, to hog the only large table in the establishment was not on. Normally, he'd bide his time at another table until his party grew large; only then would he – very politely – ask the woman to allow them access. This, however, was not a *normal* evening.

He approached with the intention of displaying his rare but memorable brusqueness. It went against his grain, but the politically correct, anything-goes attitude nurtured a bumper crop of resentment in Douglas Newman.

As he drew near, the dim light spilled over the woman's blond tresses creating an alluring frame for an unexpectedly attractive face. He recognized the perfect nose and the perfect chin. Her visage was puffier than in former times, but – despite her added weight – there could be no mistaking Clem Atwater, Tommy Dunn's "number-one girl."

Ellie Miller, the producer of *Remember When*, begged Clem for years to come out of retirement and participate. Clem wasn't interested. Of all the times for her to relent, this was the least propitious. She was, likely, closer to Tommy than anyone other than his late mother. Doubtless, she was on the train for Gloucester when the news broke. By the time she arrived . . .

He set his glass down preparatory to taking an adjacent chair. Clem looked up at him with unmistakable resentment. Her eyes flashed; she was prepared to fling a rude remark. Alas, she recognized Newman. Instead of snapping at him, she resumed her Buddhist pose.

"To tell you how sorry I am is futile," Douglas reported while taking a seat. "My condolences, Clem. I knew how much he meant to you – to us all."

She sniffed and wiped her eyes with a hankie. She'd been crying quietly – not into her beer, she had none, nor into her untouched wine.

"I didn't want to come," she squeaked. "Tommy kept telling me it would be fun; I'd have the time of my life, he said. He was so happy when I agreed. He invited himself to breakfast just last week. He was always inviting himself over, but he ate next to nothing. He liked playing with the kids. He was down on his hands and knees, just like the old days when they were little, playing like he always had. When they left for school, he chatted with Jeff an' me for a bit. He seemed happy – just fine."

She stared into her wine. Newman made no effort to break the spell. He felt Tommy's death as deeply as Clem. This would be the worst live program in the history of radio.

"I was nineteen when he geared up for his review," she continued, softly. "He rang me up and chatted away – he was so charming. It was two or three minutes before I could think to ask who it was. He said he'd spoken with my – you did the show in Leeds last week?"

Newman nodded. The Beeb and the producer thought this year's series should go on the road. They, habitually, did an annual program from the Edinburgh Festival making them skilled in remote broadcasts. It was good publicity and made the program more accessible to the public.

"I – I tried to cancel out late last week," she confessed. "I didn't want to do it. I came here knowing I'd have a miserable time, but I had no idea."

Newman took a much-needed swallow of his scotch. It braced him only slightly. Clem returned to her memories.

"He asked me to meet him for lunch. I was reticent of men chatting me up over the phone, so I checked with my dance mentor. She assured me this was on the up and up, so I met him at this posh place near the Embankment. He charmed the nervousness right out of me. We talked about everything except dancing. That was my audition – can you believe? He hired me on the spot and instructed me to be at the studio next morning at seven."

Newman nodded. He'd seen the review. It lasted only a month, at Tommy's insistence. It was a smash; it could have run for years, but Tommy hated working in front of live audiences. Though amiable enough with the *Remember Wheners*, he habitually came down with serious stage fright prior to a show. Once he got going, he was fine. Until then, however, Newman was afraid Tommy would either bolt or throw up.

"He hated live work," Clem confirmed. "He was such a perfectionist. He wanted everything EXACT. During the review, he designed an ambitious dance number. It was set to opera music –"

"I know it," Newman broke in. "I remember it after all these years! That *was* ambitious!"

Clem nodded and dabbed her eyes once more.

"I – messed up the end and spoiled it. I was sure I'd be fired. If I wasn't, I'd quit in shame. It was the worst moment of my life – until now."

"Didn't he stop the show? I thought I heard he had."

Clem nodded and sniffed.

"After the number, we were to clear the stage and change into our next costume. Tommy ordered us to stay on stage. We were petrified. We never did anything unrehearsed, and there we were, standing in front of a theatre audience without any excuse for being there. But Tommy – oh God! Dear, dear, darling Tommy just stepped up to the apron – You know what the critics say, Tommy never met a joke he didn't steal. Maybe, but he was the greatest ad-lib comedian ever. He had the audience in stitches and made us girls so relaxed, if bewildered. Finally, he came to the point. He said they'd all paid good money to see the show, and he wanted them to get their money's worth, so – I will never forget this! He explained how we'd worked so very hard on this number. "*now the girls have their breath back, we're doing it again – just for Clementine.*"

She had a brief but cathartic cry. After dabbing her eyes once more, she took a deep breath and continued.

"I wanted to hide in a deep hole," she confessed. "At the same time, my love and admiration for the man was never greater. If he told me to reach for the stars, I'd have grabbed without thinking."

"I know he was a great ad-lib comedian," Newman acknowledged. "Week after week he amazed us all with his erudition and his funny, funny stories."

Clem forced a smile. It was brief. It was for Tommy.

"When we were filming the show, we seldom did more than three takes. Because Tommy wanted perfection, we worked our asses off – not because he was boss and signed our pay cheques. We did it because he was Tommy. He performed for the world; we performed for him."

Finally, she reached for her wine. Newman gulped down the last of his drink; she took a lady-like sip of hers.

"During the run of the show, whenever a dancer stumbled or flubbed, Tommy would calmly say *Once more, just for Clem*. After that first time on stage, he never pointed his finger at the guilty one. He knew me so well by then – and he respected me. Whenever he said *Once more, just for Clem*, it was understood that one of *my* girls – he always called the dance troupe "Clem's girls" – whenever someone dropped a clangor, he refused to call them out in front of the others. *Once more, just for Clem*. Never again did he embarrass us by fingering us. He always said "just for Clem," you know, like I was the one with the whip. No scolding, no derision, no finger pointing; he'd spotted a mistake and left it to us to correct it. That is just one of the millions of reasons we loved him."

She fiddled with her wine glass for several, uncomfortable moments.

"I can't do this show," she concluded.

"You're fantastic," he assured. "The whole world would love hearing that story. I think we'll dedicate this program to remembering Tommy. We all knew him or, at least, his work. There must be thousands of stories. I, for one, want to hear them all."

She never liked the name *Clementine* and often, mildly, scolded her parents. It never occurred to her to change it as show biz people frequently did. Instead, she settled for a diminutive. It carried masculine connotations. Since she viewed herself physical for her size and weight, Clem found it acceptable.

When she first met Tommy at an up-scale restaurant, she was overwhelmed by the venue and her potential employment. She never asked about the money, and Tommy never mentioned it. Though he was nowhere near the celebrity he became, he was a shining star; working for him would punch her ticket. In her life after Tommy Dunn, Clem had a considerable prestige lever.

Lunch was first class, as one would expect. To be hired on the spot was a jaw dropper. It was, however, typically Tommy. He trusted his friends. When one of them recommended an actor, singer or dancer, he considered the vetting process complete. Since no one ever promoted a bum steer, Tommy didn't require demonstrations.

Clem half expected an invitation to audition on her back. She'd have refused and returned to the mines where perpetual obscurity was an odds-on favorite. Tommy didn't give her the opportunity to refuse. It was the first of many gestures that endeared him to her.

She was expected to be punctual. Clem did not disappoint. She reported to the rehearsal hall ten minutes prior to the seven o'clock deadline. She expected to change, at once, into her leotards and report to the chorographer for instructions. Instead, she found herself seated at a table with four other dancers. They were served a light breakfast, complements of "the boss."

At ten minutes after seven, exactly, Tommy appeared and greeted each girl by name. He chatted, briefly, with them. He asked about their health. Did they get enough sleep? Were they ready to work? Was there anything they needed? If he knew them well enough, he asked after their families. After schmoosing, he set off to rehearse with the comic actors and actresses.

That first day was exhausting! Clem claimed she danced more in the first ten-hour session than she had during her entire life to that point. It was hyperbole, of course, but she gained a great deal of respect for Tommy's exacting standards. Every step, movement, and gesture had to be perfect! To slave like a beast of burden with a smile all the while was taxing.

They were expected to perform four routines in the review. That first day, they learned (and perfected) one half of a three-minute routine.

The next morning, Tommy arrived at exactly ten minutes after seven to make the social rounds once more. One of the girls got hurt the day before – not seriously, but enough to answer him honestly when Tommy asked how she felt.

"I want the doctor to have a look at you."

"I don't need a doctor," the girl insisted.

"Maybe, not," he replied, "but the doctor will make *me* feel better."

That was Tommy.

"Where do your parents live, Clem?"

"In Milton-Keynes, sir."

He smiled.

"I'm Tommy. You're Clem. No one here is knighted. Okay?"

That was Tommy.

Even after obtaining his knighthood, Tommy refused to wear it. If you were his friend, he was Tommy. If you weren't his friend, he didn't give a damn what you called him.

She was employed for the duration of the review. The money was princely, according to the needs of a nineteen-year-old. However, since she performed for Tommy Dunn, she quickly landed a job in a West-end musical. The work was taxing but fun.

Three months into the run, Tommy called.

"Clem, can we have lunch?"

"I have to be at the theatre by four, Tommy."

"Great! I'll meet you at the Savoy at one. I will, personally, get you to the church on time."

As expected, it was another audition. During their grazing at a posh, London eatery, he abandoned the normal chit-chat.

"I've got a television show. We start work next month. Would you like to work for me?"

For a dozen, unforgettable years, she appeared on *Completely Dunn*, excepting for a portion of her first pregnancy.

She started as a dancer. Soon, she was the lead dancer. Despite her lack of musical aptitude, she sang with the other girls when Tommy told her to sing. Then, he worked her into some sketches. By the sixth season, Clem's face was as familiar to the public as Tommy's. In fact, whenever he mentioned his show, he called it *Partly Dunn, Partly Atwater.*

Rumors abounded, of course. Tommy's sexy entourage, the tabloids insisted, were couch selected and Clem was the lead mistress. Such stories fed the tabloids for years during the show and continued after its cancelation. Whenever Tommy visited Clem, her husband and their children, they enjoyed many a chuckle over the published slanders.

In truth, the only snogging Clem and Tommy did was during the filming of a sketch. In all their years together, as employer and employee, as friends, as co-stars, Clem never heard one reliably sourced story of Tommy shagging any of "his" girls. She and her husband, Jeff, theorized that Tommy was gay or had plumbing problems. There was never an indication he was gay, so they substituted mental problems as a likely reason.

Clem didn't care to know why Tommy lived alone, or why he never married, why he had no children or – as far as anyone knew – why he never dated. He was completely dedicated to his work. He wrote all his material, including lyrics and music. This accounted for twenty-seven hours of work a day. In addition, he spoke Spanish like a Spaniard, French like a Frenchman, and German like a Bavarian (he thought the dialect was "cute.")

Atop all this, he was an ancient history expert. Whenever he appeared on *Remember When*, the producers made certain there was a topic specifically for Tommy. He "remembered" things about ancient Greece, Egypt and Rome that many scholars didn't know. Most people suspected that Tommy made it all up. When persnickety listeners researched these esoteric topics, they learned that Tommy "bloody-well knew" the facts. True, he inserted cute little asides, not simply to be funny, but as a diversion to an otherwise dry-as-dust lecture.

He was a remarkable man and the truest friend Clem ever had. He never forgot a birthday. Not only did he send a gift, a token really, he would phone his birthday wishes. Even after the show was ditched, he'd show up to participate in family birthdays. Over time, he became very close to Jeff and the kids (all of whom called him Uncle Tommy).

The family laughed and enjoyed the *Completely Dunn* rebroadcasts and treasured his friendship.

When the show was pulled, Clem got dozens of offers from high-quality sources. She was sorely tempted. An established star, Clem could have become a featured player on stage, in the movies or on the telly. Alas, Tommy would no longer serve breakfast, or chat, or run lines with her in the back of a taxi (he never owned or drove a car). After much reflection and lengthy discussions with her husband, Clem realized a career in show business which did not include Tommy Dunn was not worth having.

She took most of her "pile," and opened a dance studio. When Tommy began fundraising for children's charities, Clem joined in. The tabloids insisted she was bucking to become Dame Clem. She wasn't taken in by that tripe. If Tommy became a sewer inspector, she'd become one herself, just for the opportunity (and fun) of working with him. Next to her husband and children, Tommy was the dearest person in Clem's universe.

Douglas Newman picked up his empty glass before remembering it was empty. He was tempted to get a refill but fought the urge. One more drink would not be enough. Aside from the risk of making a public spectacle of himself, Newman realized he needed a clear head and a keen mind to navigate the remainder of the evening. The catharsis achieved by crying their eyes out over Tommy's passing wouldn't help. They had a live broadcast the following afternoon. It was his job as the chairman to set the tone and provide the BBC with a quality program.

"Darling, let me tell you what, may be, my favorite Tommy story," he began.

Political correctness be damned. Douglas addressed women as "darling." From his mother to Clem's precocious daughter, every female was "darling." It was a habit he picked up at university, and he refused to abandon it for the sake of the latest linguistic fashion.

Clem was dabbing her eyes again. As hard as Tommy's death was for him, it was ten times worse for Tommy's "number-one girl."

"I was making a presentation at the National Gallery one, horrible October day. Tommy knew about it and came. When it was over, he pulled me aside and introduced me to some poor man dripping wet from the rain."

Tommy had a thousand-watt smile. He wore that smile on the afternoon when he flagged down his good friend, Douglas. The man at his side removed his sodden hat, but his raincoat was wet through. He should have looked distraught; instead, he looked as happy as Tommy himself.

"This is my friend, Henry," he announced. "He recognized me clear across the square and ran like hell just to say hello. Henry, this is Douglas."

It was always first name-only with Tommy.

"I'm in London on business," the rumpled wreck informed. "Of course, I'm a big fan. My family will be thrilled when I tell them I talked with the great Tommy Dunn – and, of course, the world-famous Douglas Newman."

There was a noticeable if unidentifiable accent accompanying the complement. Newman was uncomfortable about his fame; he was grateful for it, but never felt he deserved it. He shook the man's hand. The grip was sure. Gratitude flowed through the length of his arm.

"I'm treating Henry to light nosh at Marty's. Join us, please."

There was nothing Douglas liked less than cafeteria food. Further, eating in the crypt of St. Martin-in-the-Fields wasn't his notion of a cheery venue – particularly on a blustery, rainy, miserable day. Nevertheless, this was important to Tommy, a man difficult to turn down.

"Can you believe it?" Tommy asked of Douglas. "Henry and I both served with supply units in Normandy."

Douglas knew that Tommy served in the army as a supply sergeant. It was the part of his life he seldom discussed. "War," as he was wont to say, "is a horrible business and not to be glorified or encouraged."

Mark you, Tommy never fired a shot in anger. He hit the beach on D-plus-one and helped get petrol, rations and replacement equipment to the combat troops. Nevertheless, he saw enough to revolt him. A man whose life was dedicated to producing laughter kept his war-time experiences under wraps. Still, there he stood, grinning like the Cheshire Cat because he'd discovered a war buddy.

"You participated in the invasion?" Newman asked when the conversation stalled.

"Not exactly," the man replied. "My actual name is Heinrich. We were trying to stop it."

Clem coughed and let go with a heart-wrenching moan.

Thomas Hardy's "The Man He Killed" in reverse. Two soldiers who might, once, have shot at each other, were going to lunch. For certain, Tommy paid.

"That is so Tommy!" Clem blubbered.

Clive Martin was, arguably, the best and most prolific living figure in the comedic arts. He started out as an actor, but he (and the critics) agreed that Clive lacked the intangibles so vital for stardom. Granted, he enjoyed flashes of success, but he never became a household name (like Tommy Dunn). He might have made a good living nibbling way at the fringes of the business. Indeed, he might have carved out a comfortable niche in film and telly. Fortunately, he recognized his limitations and shifted gears.

For a decade, he wrote brilliant material for three of the country's greatest comics. Unlike Tommy Dunn who wrote and performed only his own material, a top comic trio relied on Clive to put words in their mouths. Clive satiated their needs. He could write slapstick, satire, and subtle humor to match the persona of his clients. He, also, excelled at gag writing, though this was not his favorite work.

As a bit player and character actor in films, he learned the craft. Soon enough, he thought in terms of camera angles, lighting, and sets. Eventually, he translated this interest in the subtle side of comedy that he lobbied for a career change. Under his inspired direction, Martin and a veteran stable of actors churned out eight brilliant films that, over time, became classics.

It was not until he became a regular on *Remember When* that he achieved household-name status.

During their tenure on the program, Tommy and Clive were joined at the hip. Though his program was axed years before, Tommy continued studying comedy. They often sat at a pub table long after the others retired in preparation for the following day's broadcast.

One expected two great comedic minds to howl with incessant laughter. However, Tommy and Clive were as sober as architects, speaking in low, guarded tones about visual effects. Tommy's oft repeated comment during these late-night colloquies was "I wish I'd thought of that."

Despite *Completely Dunn* being imprisoned in history, Tommy, the perfectionist, continued to discover ways and means to make his highly acclaimed cannon even better. If ever he had an opportunity to revive the show, he'd tweak the writing very little, but there'd be major changes in sets and lighting.

Tommy was addicted to light. The most frequent complaint among Dunn's cast was that the studio sets were "so bleeding hot!" Even Clem's scantily clad dancers suffered. Under Clive Martin's tutelage, Tommy, belatedly, learned the art of lighting "textures." Some scenes had greater impact with clever variations of lighting.

"Less is more," was Tommy's greatest peeve.

"Less is more?" he'd bellow. "Then nothing is everything, ain' it?"

Only under Clive's expert instruction did Tommy come to understand the concept of subtleness.

Linda Smythe was once the darling of West-end musicals. She compiled more hits and awards than any thespian without a trans-Atlantic reputation. There was a reason: she was a slave to the theatre. Rarely did she appear on telly – and never in films. Where Tommy couldn't perform well before an audience, Linda couldn't work without one.

Director after director tore their hair out during rehearsals because Linda had all the stage presence of a rusty nail. Walk throughs were tediously dull; her voice was listless; her singing tentative.

"Wait until there are arses in the seats," she'd shrug.

The more daring directors would scruff up people from the streets or invite a school outing into the rehearsal venues. If Linda knew there were people in the audience, no matter how few, she became a powerhouse of charm, wit, personality and emotion. No one fell asleep during a Linda Smythe performance.

Her theatre days were far behind her when she joined *Remember When.* She had the chops still, but Linda was a grandmother and refused to pretend otherwise. She never submitted to even minor cosmetic surgery, never took pains with her "street clothes," and never pretended to be the grand dame. She remains one of the few major entertainment personalities who can wander around Edenborough Festival venues without being recognized – not even by *paparazzi.*

Not until she joined the regulars on *Remember When*, did she enjoy an audience beyond theatre doors. She continued to perform live, but age and appearance relegated her to minor roles. Linda cared not. Her life was focused on her husband, family and the grandchildren she spoiled mercilessly. In short, she was a Tommy Dunn type of person; her life revolved around people and an ever-expanding circle of friends.

Linda lived with her husband, an epicurean restaurateur, in Hemel Hempstead. They had a "quaint" but unostentatious suburban home in a "quant" suburban neighborhood. When not working, Linda began her day by having neighbor women over for coffee and a chin wag. For her, *Remember When* was keeping "one foot in" and, thus, postponing "retirement."

Linda was Douglas Newman's gold mine. Her reminiscing about her legendary theatrical career was fascinating. Unlike others, she didn't need to embellish or make up stories about treading the boards. Moreover, she'd learned useful cooking skills from her husband of thirty-two years. (She was, by her own admission, a rotten cook; whenever they ate at home, "hubby rustled up the grub.")

Linda and Clive met up prior to entering. Doubtless, they exchanged thoughts about Tommy's recent demise. They may have devised a strategy for dealing with Clem. Whether she was inside or soon to arrive, Clem was their greatest concern. She and Tommy remained very close, and his death was sure to weigh heavy.

Despite her sorrow, Clem recognized the theatrical icon instantly. Unhesitatingly, she got to her feet as is fitting for a lowly peasant in the presence of royalty. This allowed Linda to gather the woman into a warm, heartfelt, embrace.

"I'm so very, very sorry," she sobbed. "Your pain must be excruciating. All I can say is that I share it – if that's a comfort."

"Thank you," Clem replied, barely audible.

Reluctantly, the women parted allowing Douglas the opportunity to introduce Clive Martin. To everyone's surprise, Clem leaned across the table and extended her hand. Nonplussed, Clive took it.

"An honor to meet you at last," she said. "Tommy spoke of you, often."

A moment later, she dabbed her eyes again.

"I'm so sorry," she whimpered. "I can't stop crying. You'd think all the water would be used up, but the tears keep coming and coming. Can people cry themselves to death?"

This rhetorical question left them flummoxed. Slowly, reluctantly, the standing trio slowly pulled out chairs and settled, uncomfortably, into them.

Newman cleared his throat.

"Let me bring you something," he stammered.

Normally, individuals fetched their own refreshments and paid as they went. This was not a normal gathering, however. Everyone was desperately trying to stumble through the realization that Tommy Dunn would not be joining them.

"Brandy," Linda said, using a knuckle to brush away a tear. "A large one."

"Neat whiskey," Clive said, his voice very flat.

Douglas bowed slightly at the waist before shuffling off to the bar.

The pall was oppressive. Clem's question remained on the table. No one knew how to sweep it away. Clem, however, was a trouper, as Tommy Dunn would attest. She realized she'd committed an egregious error. It was her place to make amends.

She sniffed and turned toward the legend she'd met for the first time.

"May I ask you something that's bothered me for years?"

Linda was stymied. She knew Clem only as Tommy's faithful Tonto. At that moment, however, and under the circumstances, there was no way she could deny the girl anything. From Linda's perspective, Clem would, forever, be Tommy's "sassy little lassie." Had Clem asked for the loan of a hundred-thousand quid, Linda hadn't power to bicker.

"Ask away," she replied, warily.

"How did you put up with that obnoxious Gilbert Collinsworth?"

The tears temporarily abated due to a flash of temper.

"*Obnoxious*, darling?"

Linda couldn't help it. She was stunned and fell back on Newman's favorite endearment for lack of anything cogent.

"How many times did he say *We should never have women on this show; it ruins the intellectual integrity of the program*? He was brutal. I'd have slapped his face."

Linda couldn't stop herself. She laughed. It was genuine. It was her first moment of felicity since learning of Tommy's departure.

"That was part of his schtick," she reported. "He pestered me for years to come on the show. He practically dragged me into the studio. I never would have joined up if not for Gil. He was a dear friend."

Clem wasn't convinced.

"He said terrible things about you," she remined.

"And never meant a word," Linda insisted.

Clem sat back. She'd not make an issue, but, obviously, she was unconvinced. Linda sensed the latent umbrage and took a breath.

"Tommy's show, particularly in the early years, was labeled *knickers comedy*. Despite having you parade about in your scanties, did he ever do or say anything to you that made you think he was disrespectful?"

Clem didn't have to ponder that. Tommy never asked his girls to do anything they didn't want or think proper. Sexual inuendo was fine, but Clem wasn't the only one who politely declined to step into a costume or participate in a sketch she felt was objectionable or demeaning. Tommy never twisted arms. He trusted the judgement of his employees. If they expressed discomfort over the show's content, he relented without pouting and without rancor.

"Never!" she assured.

Linda placed her hands on the table and turned up her palms.

"There it is."

Clive seized the opportunity.

"Of course, you couldn't see it on the radio," he added. "Linda would be quaking with laughter whenever Gil started one of his stupid-women rants. It got laughs precisely because everyone knew it was an act."

Clem thought for a moment longer.

"Once, Tommy sent me back to wardrobe because he thought my skirt was too short for the skit we were filming," she recalled. "He was very coy when we were dressed – ah – *undressed* on the set. I – guess – I understand you – now."

Clive squirmed uncomfortably in his seat and cleared his throat again.

"Many people, now days, are conditioned to look for social or political subtexts in everything. That's why people daren't laugh. It's exactly why *Remember When* is so important. We present face-value comedy. If you analyze every nuance, humor flies away."

"*On winged words*, as Tommy would say."

Linda hated political dogma. Clive was getting preachy, and, as much as she liked him, she was determined to shut him down.

"An overdose of sleeping pills," she injected hurriedly. "The police said nothing about finding a note. Do you think it was intentional?"

Clem braced. Horrible thoughts swirled in her head since the news reached her. She managed to keep them at bay but hadn't succeeded in ostracizing them. She drew in a lung-full of air and cast a glance at the gentleman on her left.

"I got out of the business because I could," she began. "I have a family. Tommy – well, he never drank, smoked, did drugs or cavorted with loose women. Show business was his family. He had his work and his sleeping pills."

"Please," Linda interrupted politely. "Don't go there. I'm satisfied it was accidental."

Clem took up her wine glass with a steady hand. She took her first appreciative sip of the evening.

Tommy, the perfectionist, took an *accidental* overdose? Not bloody likely!

She flashed back to the show and how, the moment the director yelled "cut," he often doubled up with laughter. She recalled the terror Tommy exhibited before stepping in front of a live audience. She recalled how solicitous he was about everyone's health – not just the performers, but everyone in the crew.

They ruminated quietly until Douglas returned with the drinks. Clive dispatched his whiskey with one, greedy gulp. Linda, in contrast, was in no hurry to start on her brandy.

"I'm sure James will join us shortly," Douglas said to fill the conversational void.

Indeed, the fourth "contestant" might not arrive until just before the show

– if then. Someone had to take Tommy's place at the, preverbal, last minute. The producers dispatched an infrequent guest player from Cardiff. Theoretically, the travel distance was not great, but "hey-you" situations are seldom clean.

"It's a ruddy cheek, I know," Clem advanced with a calm, clear voice. "May I make a request?"

"What is it, darling?"

"Could we dispense with the audience tomorrow afternoon? I'm sure they'll understand. The four of us could sit around, with you, of course, and exchange memories of Tommy. I'm sure we'd get a lot of laughs. The people listening at home will too."

Douglas Newman didn't need to think very hard.

"I'm sure we could arrange it," he said, realizing he'd insist upon it.

The people at Bush House would understand the extenuating circumstances. Even if they didn't, he'd collected many chips during his quarter-century chairmanship of the program.

"Could we, please, change the program title to *Remember Tommy*?"

She'd stopped crying.

Mark Williams

Lockdown

Massa Missy Ma'am directed her slaves to return to their cabins and remain inside until the Passover Virus passed – um – over. At the time, no one knew how many decades we'd be sequestered by edict. Indeed, the "experts" were so baffled by this malady that they hadn't a clue. They issued "guesses" for weeks. Massa Missy Ma'am didn't guess; she issued dictates.

Unfortunately, our plantation owner was a couple decades late. Believe me, there was a time when I'd have leapt for joy.

"Please, Massa Missy Ma'am: Don' throw me in de briar patch!"

I'd, gleefully, retire to my slave hovel and hunker down for however long it took Massa Missy Ma'am to think of (dream up) something else. Just keep the power on or give me access to batteries. I'd be as happy as a kid in a swimming hole.

I started out with a radio my parents got as a wedding gift. When TV became a staple, the radio was transformed into a room ornament. I commandeered it from time to time because there was a receptacle for my 45-rpm record player jack. The radio became a speaker. I played the short stack of records time and again as background noise.

Somehow, I got interested in the radio itself. I recall listening to music. I remember the jingle and music of a brewery no longer in existence. It may have been in search of music when I began moving the dial. Suddenly, I heard "Gunsmoke!"

Cool!

I was about to hear a program I, and my parents, watched regularly.

Yuk!

Matt Dillon's voice was not James Arness. Keep turning that dial.

Isn't it interesting to turn the dial? There are so many things one discovers. First among these was the discovery that I could get more stations after dark. Additionally, not all stations came in clear and unencumbered. There were some stations speaking *not* English. When I visited relatives in Ohio, I was excited to hear stations in New York! By this time, I could recognize Spanish at home, I discovered, in Ohio, I could recognize French!!

My uncle was an amateur radio operator (W8DDG, silent key; the call sign has since been reassigned). I sat for hours at his side while he sipped Martinis and chatted up other HAMs. I couldn't understand Morse, but my uncle kept me informed as to the locations of those he messaged. When my uncle and his "contact" spoke via microphones, it was a treat.

For some reason, I spent the night with Uncle Frank and Aunt Bea. My cousin was living and working in Arizona, but his bedroom was converted into station W8DDG. The bed, however, was still there. It was mine for the night.

Being in the same room with hundreds (perhaps, thousands) of dollars of radio equipment was too tempting. When satisfied Uncle Frank and Aunt Bea were asleep, I plugged in earphones and fired up the radio. I'd watched Uncle Frank change bands and noted how he tuned.

Magic!

I heard radio amateurs from all over America and elsewhere. Most were very near, but some were from California, Mexico, Texas and, even, Costa Rica.

My heartrate soared higher than a cat's back. I was operating an instrument that spanned thousands of miles.

Then –

A voice – in English – English with an accent!

This was no HAM. This man was an announcer. A radio station announcer. How did I stumble onto a broadcast station? Curiosity made me tarry.

Then –

"This is Radio Australia, the overseas service of the ABC."

This, I decided, was more interesting than anything to date. Unfortunately, the station was signing off.

Damn!

Well, I knew there was someone in Australia willing and able to talk to me. I wasn't, however, ready to become a HAM. My parents couldn't afford the equipment. I certainly couldn't. However, I had (what I later learned) the DX bug.

DX is radio jargon for "distance."

Reunited with an ancient (to me), disused wedding gift, I began DXing. I had a wall map of the United States in my room. I bought straight pins and made little pennants. Whenever I caught a station ID, I'd make a pennant, inscribe the call letters, and stick in the correct location on the map. Within weeks, my tiny flags marched across the Mississippi. Des Moines, Chicago and New Orleans were regular visitors in my unofficial monitoring station.

Every night was an adventure. More than that, I picked up and recorded little bits and bobs for use at school. Jokes were a prized commodity, but I gleaned items of interest which didn't, otherwise, make it into the provincial homes of Roseburg, Oregon. These I would parcel out to teachers, during class. I imagined that my fellow students were in awe of my intellectual largess.

(They probably weren't, but imagination was an integral feature of my DXing.)

Cousin Jimmy, in whose room I was when I tuned in Radio Australia, came to visit. He was stationed at Ft. Lewis and spent part of his leave with us. He and I chatted several times in my room. He saw my map and asked about my pennant collection. I, enthusiastically, told him.

At some point, I caught my father and Jimmy having a chin wag in the living room. When I entered, they ceased talking. My dad told me (*told* mind you) to leave the house. I considered that both abrupt and rude. I wasn't happy, and I showed it. I was curious, of course, but mostly, I was mad.

That Christmas, I found myself the owner of a brand-new Air-o-Ear – a cheap commercial receiver with a neat band switch on the face. I could select LF (low frequency), AM (my natural DX hunting ground), MF (medium frequency), HF (high frequency), and VHF (very high frequency).

After I'd been kicked out of the house, Jimmy told my father about how he could secure a multi-band radio at a price the family could afford. This was long before Amazon, of course, and ordering by mail was generally the turf of Roger Ripoff and his cousins. Jimmy convinced my dad that the radio offer was legit.

It was worth a million dollars to me. I could eavesdrop on radio amateurs (I listened for but never heard Uncle Frank), monitor anyone using the airport frequency, and – best of all – I got to hear Radio Australia again.

I bought a world map. It was soon decorated with a bevy of pennants. Pin holes were occupying Melbourne, Tokyo, Hilversum (Holland), Cologne, Stockholm, Cairo, Montreal, Oslo, Moscow, Havana, Auckland, London, Lisbon, Madrid, Prague, Bucharest, Peking (back in the day), and sundry other locations.

On school days, I would rush home and tune in the Voice of America Magazine Show, a forerunner of NPR (but without the political bias). I'd set my alarm clock for four in the morning so I could listen to 6WN from Perth, Australia. This station had news, music and entertainment shows that got every day off to a great start.

I was very excited when I captured Radio New Zealand. They had radio serials on weekends. Radio Nederland had a music request program (they played no few of my requests). Keith Glover, on Radio Australia, replied to three or four missives I posted to their Mail Bag *Programme*. I got radio guides from five or six broadcasters; I read and re-read them several times.

When I left for college, my Air-O-Ear went with me. Around noon, daily, I made certain to listen to Radio Moscow because it played twenty or more uninterrupted minutes of captivating folk music. The Voice of America Jazz Hour and Music USA were two other favorite shows.

Inevitably, I developed my favorites among the corps of announcers. Cheryl Riggins (Finland), Elizabeth Blaine (Austria), Larry Wayne (Germany), Willis Conover (Voice of America), and Peter Michael Black (Brazil) to name but a few. They were welcome anytime.

Two people were special. A man with a rich baritone voice, Jeffery (?) Godfrey (I called him "Golden Throat") was a regular news reader and features host at Radio Portugal. I would check in to hear if he were announcing. If not, I dialed in another station. The second person was never identified by name. She was a news reader for RAI (Italy). The club magazines dubbed her "The Dead Lady." Her English was good enough, but her trademark was a listless monotone.

When I relocated to Europe, my Air-O-Ear was a fond memory. After years of abuse, it was replaced by two (even cheaper) devices in quick succession. They kept me in touch with the BBC, both the World Service and AM stations, and the "regulars" I often logged in when still in America.

I met a woman serving an internship with Deutsche Welle in Bonn (moving into the vacated offices when the federal government took everything back to Berlin). I enjoyed listening to her on the air. There is a photo of her holding up a DW mic as if she were interviewing me. I keep this picture prominently displayed.

She escorted me into the building. She gave me the grand tour of the facility. I noted the numerous conference rooms were glassed in.

"This used to be the *Bundestag* complex," she reminded. "After the Nazi Era, people put up glass walls to discourage secret meetings. As you walk down this hall, you can look in and see what people are doing."

I wondered if I could meet Larry Wayne. Alas, he was gone long before my friend landed her internship, but she promised to ask her boss. Later, she informed me that Larry married a Swedish woman. When he reached retirement age, they relocated to a small estate in Sweden.

This same intern invited a friend and me to celebrate Thanksgiving in Bonn. The assembly was so huge, the venue was an empty garage. Many people from many nations were invited from the DW workplace. The Kosovo mess was full-speed-ahead at the time. Our hostess, deliberately, seated an Albanian and a Serb next to each other. They, and everyone else, got along swimmingly.

It was the first Thanksgiving I experienced which was nearest the intent of the original celebration.

One year, the BRT had an "open house." I sent in a request and was issued a pass. I trained to Brussels and paid for two nights in a nice hotel. I reported to the specified place at the specified time. A young lady, in a gorgeous, orange BRT t-shirt hurried to the gate to check my ID and escort me in. Only a dozen or so guests attended, so we enjoyed considerable face time with on-air personalities. The staff allowed us to sit *in the studio* during a live news broadcast directed to the Middle East.

A young lady employee made the rounds. When she introduced herself, I felt like a fraud. I was not a "frequent" listener to the BRT since arriving in Europe. I didn't recognize her by either voice or name; information I was hesitant to share with her.

No fear. She was doing the PR bit and wasn't fishing for adulation. However, during our brief colloquy, she related a precious anecdote.

"My parents," she informed, "are missionaries in India *and* avid DXers. They were thrilled when I told them about my job here. They make certain to listen to my feature whenever they can. One day, on my way to work, I had a flat. I called in, and they had someone else tape my segment. When it aired, the head of the English service got a phone call from India. My father wanted to know what had happened to his darling daughter."

One would think that I had forsaken DXing for SWLing (short wave listening). True, I once followed *Letter from America* around the world, beginning with the BBC World Service and finishing up, several countries later, in New Zealand. Obviously, I had my favorite stations and programs. However, I continued to surf the bands.

When the Army sent me to Europe, I enjoyed listening to Bucharest, Sofia, and RIAS (Radio in the American Sector) from Berlin with regularity. I really enjoyed listening to the ten-minute English broadcast from Surinam. A station in Malta (affiliated with Libya) had very entertaining programs on weekends. Radio Jordan was another, very special, favorite. They rebroadcast a bevy of BBC "oldies" (*My Word*, a special favorite, and *Just a Minute*). Additionally, Jordan had locally produced programs. I was riveted by reports of archeology in Jordan, especially the Roman digs. I also enjoyed their music programs (mostly Western and much of it American, and all of it of by-gone days: Henri Mancini, Brenda Lee just as examples).

The greatest comedy show on shortwave was from Radio Albania. The "news broadcasts" from this station had me in stitches. It was so brazenly dericulous! Why they bothered with English transmissions remains a mystery. I guess, they were so excited to share their weird and dark visions that they never considered the audience. A favorite of mine was the program relating the bloody, people's struggle to preserve the Albanian language (either that, or another feature about copper-wire production in the South Albania). This kind of "journalism" died out in the 90s, but it is making a comeback in the new century, particularly America and Western Europe. I guess, Tirana gets the last laugh.

Tirana for laughs, but Gjirokaster, on 5030, played great classical music records. If atmospheric conditions were bad and DXing sucked, I'd tune in this seldom mentioned Albanian station and enjoy great music! If there is anyone still alive in Albania who remembers this radio anomaly, I have yet to hear of them. Even at SWL conventions and DX gatherings, I draw blank, confused expressions whenever I mention this wonderful station. It makes me feel so special; someone in the Albanian government went to a lot of trouble and expense to put a station on the air with but a single listener: me! I dare someone to prove me wrong.

HorK, my abbreviation for a station in Kiev, played a variety of uninterrupted music of all genres. The Voice of Kenya, also, featured a variety of music – just for *my* enjoyment.

My greatest thrill was picking up Port Moresby on a cheap receiver that was not designed to pick up that station's frequency. I enjoyed listening to the news in pidgin English. Similarly, I discovered the Falkland Islands after months of trying. Similarly, I, finally, picked up the only shortwave transmitter in Antarctica.

Before closing my logbook, I logged one hundred ninety countries and territories (granted, a dozen or so were relay stations).

I looked forward to retirement. It would give me more time to fish some Indonesian, low-powered station out of the mud of atmospherics and solar flares. However, satellites and the internet made shortwave obsolete. Many stations have shut down. Now, I listen to Radio Romania (one of the holdouts) on livestream.

My last log entry is both poignant and pathetic.

DATE	STATION	COMMENTS	FREQUENCY	TIME IN TIME OUT (UTC)
31 Aug (2008)	NZ	hymns, nx, jazz vocal "Just One of Those Things" At 1219 over NED tuning sig.	9655	1100 1300

Now, when I listen to Radio New Zealand, I stream the National Programme. What I wouldn't give to hear the Radio Nederland World-Wide tuning signal again.

Unfortunately, Massa Missy Ma'am's command to hide under my bed until ordered to do otherwise came over a dozen years too late. What glory my shortwave receiver and I would have experienced during solitary confinement! For certain, I would have been neither bored nor alone.

The Souvenir

We had a son once. He lived for almost an hour. The doctor wanted to "snip" Becky, but she wouldn't have it. She used language not fittin' for a woman, but she's a farm wife. Now, I never finished school, but Becky, "Rebecca" to her folks – they never liked me much – she graduated. Three weeks later, we were hitched. She was never a beauty, but she was cute and was always nice to me. I couldn't a done better, but she sure could'a. I thought I was lucky until – well, we tried again. The doctor had a fit.

We almost lost her. The baby was fine, but –

We wanted a son. In fact, we wanted a flock of sons. Farming in a county that civilization forgot is tougher than choppin' nettles in infested coveralls. Now, farmin' ain't never gonna be easy, but the more help, the less emergencies – well, at least with a half-dozen farm hands, there's always someone for to deal with a scare until we can all attend it.

We had Sharon.

Sharon ain't a boy. Becky – well, we'd not be havin' no more kids. We was both sorrowful, but for different reasons. But, Becky didn't weep too much. She loved Sharon and would bust her butt to see to her every need.

One day, Becky calls me into the house. She needed to get to the market and keep a appointment with Doc Morris (the ole quack), and she was afeared for Sharon. Usually, she took the baby with her, but there was bad weather and bad roads leadin' into town. I had a sick calf and a pump that needed attention and I had ta baby sit. Now, I was really tempted to leave Sharon to look after herself, but I promised Becky I'd do what she wanted. Maybe, I had no use for Sharon, but I wouldn't lie to Becky.

I paced around the house for however long I paced around the house. I was boiling. I needed to check on the calf. I needed to fix that damn pump, or we'd soon have an empty reservoir. Rain was nice, but it couldn't fill the water tank.

Finally, I marched right over to the crib. Sharon was gumming a fist until she saw me.

"You ain't a good idea," I told her.

Her eyes got as big as pie pans, and she started kicking her feet and waving her arms around – then she smiled. Now Becky and the quack said Sharon weren't old enough to smile, but I know what I seen. She smiled!

Now, I was mad, and I was worried, and I was a prisoner in the house when I had work to do, but – Well, Sharon knew that that damned smile – I mean, I don't care what nobody says, that little girl knew that Daddy was her toy. It wasn't the first time she pulled that stunt. I cannot count the times I was so mad at her I was ready to hit her, but that damned smile –

There oughtta be a law!

Well, Sharon grows into a cute little girl, then she turned into a pretty, young woman. She was popular at school cuz she got along with everybody. I mean, if she could buffalo her dad, well – ain't nobody else to stand a chance. And she was powerful smart. I don't know how many times her teachers said how smart she was. I was for sure that the teachers said that about everybody, but Becky took it to heart. She was all the time buyin' books for her just cuz Sharon liked to read. We couldn't afford to keep the butt blister in books, so Becky got her a library card at the county library. Between schoolbooks and library books, it weren't safe to walk around the house. I swear, I woulda tossed everyone of them damn books out the window and into the mud except –

Sharon earned her keep. She milked the cow, fed the chickens, sloped the pigs, and plowed. She wanted to read when she was on the tractor, but I wouldn't have it. Becky suggested we put a radio on the tractor to keep her from getting bored and falling asleep. That was a good idea. Sharon had to have the volume way up to hear the music over the engine noise. If I ever suspected that she was slacking, I stop doin' whatever I was doin' and listen. I could tell if the tractor was movin' or parked somers. During harvest we'd start and not stop until the crop was in. Sometimes it took thirty hours. Sometimes it took forty hours. However long it took, we'd work in shifts with Becky bringing us food and coffee so we could chew and gulp and work all 'tonce.

Becky and me treated Sharon different. I treated her like a son and farm hand. Becky treated her like a young girl. I let Becky get away with it because – well, Becky was the best thing in my life, and I wouldn't risk ruin it. Besides, Becky enjoyed having a daughter and teaching her to do all the little girlie things. So long as it didn't interfere with the farm chores, I put up with it.

Then, boys!

Now, if a boy wanted to come over and help with the chores, I treat 'em right nice. But, damn, blast and double damn, they'd want to take Becky to a show or a dance or a game. I had a shotgun I kept handy for to rid us of critters, but I was pert near usin' it against those pests who come round to pant at Sharon. The only thing to stop me was Becky.

"He's somebody's son," she'd say.

That stabbed me in the heart. I know the notion stabbed Becky bad, too. Our son, had he lived, would be three years older than Sharon. For a person that left us after only a few minutes, he sure got hold of us. I tried to tie up Sharon with after school chores to chain her down, but if some guy come round askin' for her and Sharon wanted to go with him, we let it be. Neither of us wanted to go through that "somebody's son" thing again.

I want ta make it clear, right here, if any of those little pip-squeaks hurt Sharon, there would have been a funeral right soon. I'd been a boy myself, and I know what bastards we are. But – and this here is the honest to God truth – I never treated Becky as anything other than a lady. She was a saint back in the day, and she's a saint still! Sharon deserves to be a saint, too. Anyone who thinks different will meet Papa, and it won't be for to talk.

Sharon said she wanted to go to college!

What the hell!? She started talkin' about it not long after she started high school. Now, we ain't got money enough to send her to college. She's smart enough to know that. Sharon says she can, maybe, get a scholarship. Yeah, like a farm kid is gonna get one of them! But, then, she wants to get a job so she can save up for college.

"You got a job!" I reminded. "We got a farm to run!"

Well, I don't pay wages. It took all of Becky's powers to get me to give her a weekly allowance.

"At least she isn't after us to buy her new clothes," Becky said.

Well, there was that. Sharon wasn't no clothes horse, but she made most of her school clothes herself. That was bad enough. She'd be cutting and stitching and sewing when she could have been doing chores. Becky used to get after her for not doing her homework. Somehow, Sharon seemed to get her homework done, but don't ask me how. Between farm work, sewing, and her infernal reading, there was no time for anything else – to say nothing of stepping out with some lay-about who shoulda been helping on his father's farm!

Sharon didn't much talk about school beyond a favorite teacher or a book or story she'd been assigned. She brought home good marks on her report cards which made Becky very happy. I didn't give a tinker's damn about grades, but Becky's being happy and proud meant a lot to me. So, I didn't know much about Sharon's school days until – well, until recent.

It used to aggravate me no little when I had ta help Sharon hitch somethin' to the tractor or help her lift somethin'. She couldn't buck hay worth a damn, but she'd bust a gut tryin'. I guess, maybe, I said some things that were better left unsaid. Some things probably hurt her. Well, I guess I feel kinda sorry about them things – now. At the time, and in the heat of battle, I mighta said somethin' about wantin' a son who could be more help. Sharon never said nothin'. She never let on that my cursing and fumin' got to her, but I guess it did. She gave it everything she got, but they's some things a girl, even a farm girl, can't handle. I feel bad, now. It wasn't Sharon's fault she was a girl, and I wish now that I'da said something more – well, fatherly, when she did her damndest – even if it weren't up to snuff.

Becky told me something that she heard in the bank one day from a woman who worked there and went to our church. This was after Sharon went away, so this gossip was years old. Anyways, the woman told how some boy was digging at her over somethin'. He was one of them athletes who had nothin' better to do after school but play games or practice playing games. He thought he was a real hot shot! One day, I guess, Sharon had her fill of his guff and she said somethin'. She kept on sayin' somethin' until Mr. Muscle Brain got miffed. He said somethin' like Sharon, who couldn't even do five push-ups, had no grounds to say nothin' to him about nothin'. Well, right there in class with the teacher lookin' on, Sharon lay flat on the floor, puts her left hand behind her back and whips off five, one-handed push-ups.

"I guess you're right," she said. "I guess these count as only half a push-up."

Well, sir, the class encouraged the boy to do one handed push-ups, but he had a muscle ache or somthin', so he didn't dare try right then.

How I wished Sharon hada said somethin' at the time. Becky don't much believe gossip, but she saw the teacher some days later and asked about this little tidbit. He vouched for Sharon, and that's good enough for me. Neither of us ever asked Sharon about it – well, not yet anyways.

Sharon wanted ta go to college. She worked hard and got a good scholarship. That was nice, but Sharon had made up her head she was goin' to college. She got an afternoon job in town, opened a bank account and started putting money away. I was proud of her and mad at her at the same time. She knew what she wanted, and she worked her butt off to get it. The farm was left to me. Those little, pain-in-the-ass things Sharon did to free me up for more important work were left to Dad. Becky stepped in and started doing Sharon's chores. That made me mad and sad at the same time.

"Our daughter wants to go to school," Becky told me. "I'll help her anyway I can."

I thought Sharon was spoiled and Becky was helping spoil her. I stated changin' my mind when Sharon would come home and change clothes after work. If something had been left undone, she went out, sometimes in the dark, and took care of it. Becky would bark and plead and threaten, but Sharon would not touch her food so long as something remained undid.

There's one thing that I enjoy above anything else and that's a good, hot meal in the evening. Becky made casseroles, mostly, they were cheap and good. Becky could make a great casserole out of grass and chicken feed – well, pert near, anyways. Because I thought a hot meal was my highlight of any day, my heart bled when Sharon would come in late and gulp down cold fixins. That's when I realized how much she wanted to go to college.

"If I can't afford college next year," she promised me. "I'll work a job in town to save up for the next year. I'll still help out on the farm, Pa. I promise."

I almost said what I was thinkin'. I damn near said "If you don't help on the farm, you'll sleep in the barn."

I didn't say that. For one thing, Becky would have a fit and I would be the one sleeping in the barn. There was another reason. One night, when I turned out the lights for bed, I noticed there was a glow in the living room. I was upset. Someone had left the TV on or, maybe, the kitchen light. 'Twernt neither. It was the light in Sharon's room. She was doin' her homework. I woulda said somethin' to somebody, but I was beat. I went to bed and tried not to think about it.

"Our daughter," as Becky is want to say, really, really, really wanted to go to college!!!

She got a scholarship. It was pretty dern good according to folks who knows about such. She'd need some pocket money, but she could get that offen her savings. She would see if she couldn't get a part-time job in the city and bank her pay "for a rainy day" as she say.

Well, okay. But what was it she wanted to study?

English!

Now, what the hay? In our little town, we spoke Merican which was good enough for anybody. I mean, if she wanted to study farmin' or somethin' useful, that would have been fine. But English! Oh, she wanted to study Shakespeare and read some of those high-brow books, but – damnnation! She'd read more than her share a that stuff in high school. Who would need more? I was really disappointed.

Sharon was on top of the world. So was Becky. It made me feel like I wasn't worth the time a day.

When she left, I went into her room. I'd seen it plenty enough, but I never went in. When Sharon and I had talks, I'd stand in the doorway, and she'd sit on her bed. She liked reading while laying down, but she did her homework on the kitchen table – unless she was up past civilized bedtime, then, she'd work in her room. If she needed to write or do her math, she used the floor for her desk.

It was so – weird! It was the same bed, the same closet, the same bookcase, the same bedspread, the same curtains, the same wallpaper, but it was so sad. Very sad. Damned sad.

Becky came up behind me – snuck up, more like.

"She's gone," she whispered.

In that moment, I realized that I had lost more than a part-time farm hand. I, also, experienced a terrifying vision.

After the doctors and nurses had done all they could for our baby boy, they lay him on Becky's naked stomach to exchange body heat. They tended to Becky and got her patched up, checking on baby every few moments. Finally, we heard a pathetic little sigh. Baby's hands opened and closed slowly then lay limp.

The nurse tended him and called the doctor. He felt for a pulse and checked for breathing before nodding to the nurse who wrapped the body in a blanket and carried him away.

Becky's eyes were full of tears, but she was composed – somehow.

"He's gone," she said to me as if I'd just missed the mailman.

Those words would thunder through a thousand dreams over the years. Here they were again – maybe, not exact, but I felt them right down to my bones. I don't think I ever hurt so bad. After, Sharon left for college – well, that hurt came pretty damn close to – that other time.

"I want to burn every book in the world," I told her.

"No, you don't," she said softly. "You'd never hurt our daughter by destroying those things that make her happy."

Well, I didn't say nothin', but I agreed. As frustrated and angry as Sharon could make me, I would never be so cruel as to take away things she loved.

Sharon didn't learn about her brother until her middle teens. It was the summer of hell. She walked, she talked, she did her chores, she minded her mother. However, she was surly and curt. We didn't know if she was angry with us for not telling her, angry with the world for never knowing her own brother, if she accused us of killing the poor thing, or if she was angry with God. She never told us, and we never asked.

About a year went by when she and Becky had words over some stupid nothing.

"Sharon, you need to go to your room for a while," Becky suggested.

"It isn't my room, Mama."

Sharon said it so quietly, I barely heard it in the living room, but I trembled right down to my toes. Sharon walked past me to her – place. She didn't close the door. Not knowing why, I went to the doorway and found her sitting on her bed looking out the window. I didn't say nothin' because – hell! There was nothing to say.

Eventually, she turned and looked at me. Well, not quite, she looked right through me.

"I'm sorry, Papa," she said just above a whisper. "I know, now. This was supposed to be *his* room."

Now, my hackles were up.

"You think you'd be sleeping in a lean-to out by the gas tank?"

I was pretty hot, but I kept my voice down.

"I know you'd build an addition for me," she said. "You'd probably do most of it yourself, but it would take you away from more important work and – that wouldn't be right."

She had me there. No matter what I said, it would sound either stupid or a lie. Sharon feels things – way down deep. She seldom showed it, but her brother's death really shook her up.

"Could you do me a big, big, big favor, Sharon?"

She didn't like the sound of that.

"I might – try," she said. "It depends."

"Go make up with your mother."

She stared out the window for a long while. Finally, she took in a breath – a deep breath. It was an effort, but she got to her feet.

"You owe me a big favor, Papa, and soon."

She returned to the kitchen and made nice with Becky.

Ya know, I don't recall her ever calling in that favor I owed her.

Several weeks go by. We got a letter every other day and Sharon would call every Sunday after church. Her letters were chatty, but the phone calls was expensive and short. Still, we got to hear her voice and that was a big boost going into a new week.

One day, I comes in for dinner and Becky has a expensive looking card on the table waitin' fer me. I don't notice until after I wash up and sit at table. It was a big Christmas-card-like bobber with bright colors and fancy lettering. It was from Sharon's sorority. Now, I know from nothin' about such as this, but Sharon's notes from school mentioned that one of the sororities was interested in her joinin' their club or whatever 'twas. Becky tried essplainin', but I don't think she knows about such as that either. Sharon got a job waitin' table in the evenings, and she was feeling pretty good about joinin' up since the scholarship paid for her tuition. She was addin' to the money she already got banked, so she could pay for her dorm room and any knick-knacks she fancied. It would cost a "little" more to join the sorority, but not so very much. Besides, freshmen wasn't allowed to live in the sorority itself until they'd passed their classes for a school year. Still, Sharon was in the club.

The college had a Dad's Weekend in the Fall and a Mother's Weekend in the Spring. I was invited to go up to college and be with Sharon for a Friday afternoon and Saturday. There'd be activities and such nonsense, but I could be with Sharon for a couple days. Normally, weekends were reserved for those projects I couldn't finish or get to during the week. I wasn't eager to abandon the farm, but the chance to see Sharon again was just too strong. Still, I had no business in college.

"Them snooty college folks look down on such as me," I grumbled.

"Let 'em look," Becky says. "You get to see your daughter. You get to *be* with her."

That was pretty powerful, but I really didn't want to be around all them society folks who drink tea with their pinkies in the air.

"Don't you love your daughter?" Becky asked.

That damned Becky! No matter how much I loved her, she knew which button to push. She could get me to do anything I didn't want to do. Sharon learned this from her. I might be able to get past Becky, but I couldn't resist very long if they both teamed up on me. Well, I had two-week's warning. If I put in an extra couple of hours a day, I might be able to leave the farm for a weekend without feelin' guilty about it. I didn't like workin' after supper, but – well, Becky ain't goin' to tell *me* I don't love Sharon! Besides, when Becky gets invited for Mom's Weekend, she won't have no right to beg off.

Well, that's for Spring. This was Fall, and I had an elephant on my back. College was no place for me. College people were way outside my circle. I got nervous going to church and being around the city nose-in-the-air types. Of course, there were several farm families who attended service, so I didn't have to mingle with "royalty" – not that they wanted to have any more to do with me than I wanted to schmooze with them. At college – Jesus, Lord! I'd, probably, be the only farmer there.

Becky got a good breakfast in me, but it was a battle. I was as nervous as a hound dog passing peach seeds. I wasn't hungry. Becky never allowed me to leave the house without a good breakfast under my belt. The fact that I was not headed for the fields that morning had nothing to do with it. It took her nearly an hour to coax and shame me into cleaning my plate. Finally, I set off only to return a minute later. I needed to pee. Yes, I was scared.

I drove slowly and carefully. Every mile brought me closer to a place I really didn't want to be at. I stopped once to order a coffee. I hardly touched the cup. Despite my foot-dragging, I arrived at the El Cheapo Motel two hours before Sharon promised to pick me up. I paced the room before throwing myself on the bed to rest up for my next round of pacing. There wasn't much room to pace and laying down made me uncomfortable and made me even more nervous. I took up Gideon and prayed I'd find comfort there, but the letters squirmed, and I couldn't make sense of nothing.

When the time neared, I left the room and paced around the parking lot. I heard a horn and turned to face my doom. Sharon waved to me from the passenger's seat of a beat-up Chevy sedan that may have been powered by rubber bands. When the car stopped, she rushed over to me and gave me a big hug.

That, alone, was worth the trip!

She introduced me to the driver, one of her "sisters" whose name I forgot instantly. The young girl, she looked about thirteen, smiled and said something about something. She said goodbye and Sharon said goodbye and I mumbled something – I think. The car pulled away and disappeared.

Sharon wore a shirt and jeans (she'd made them both at home).

"You must drive me to the dorm, Papa," she grinned. "I just got out of class, and I must change. We're going to a tea at the sorority. We'll be late if we don't hurry."

God, either help me or take me, now!

I'd brought my Sunday suit, but I'd need to shower and shave before changing. I panicked.

"It's informal," Sharon assured. "Just put on a tie. You'll be fine."

I'll look like a farmer – a farmer wearing a tie. Unless Sharon wore combat boots with her dress, I'd be the only laughingstock. A tea, for cryin' in a bucket! I don't even like tea. I, especially, don't like being amid a gaggle of young women. I wouldn't understand a damn thing they might talk about and, after my explainin' row crops, I'd nothing to say – nothing that would be of interest to smart college girls.

Sharon had to help me with my tie. My fingers wouldn't cooperate.

"Just be yourself, Papa," she said, soothingly. "I will introduce you to people. You will be introduced to other fathers by other daughters. Please, don't bore everyone with that story of yours – about dining with the Queen in Buckingham Palace."

She chuckled. I didn't think it was funny.

College was where I was not supposed to be.

"I don't belong here," I muttered.

"Well, maybe I don't either," Sharon said. "This is something I dreamed about, and something I've wanted for a long time. If it doesn't work out, I'll get a job back home and help on the farm."

That, I decided, sounded hopeful.

We had to park on the street about two blocks from the tea. I didn't mind. I didn't want to ruin an event by any of those fancy ladies having to look at a fifteen-year-old scrap heap. It was just fine for running into town for to buy groceries and goin' to church Sundays, but it wasn't somethin' I cared to have Sharon seen in – not with her nice dress.

The sorority was a huge, three-story mansion or had been at one time – maybe. Sharon led me to the biggest door I'd ever seen – it was two inches thick of the most no-nonsense wood I ever saw. Sharon turned the big silver nob and walked in like she owned the damn place. Inside was the biggest living room I ever saw. There was three family-sized couches and a sofa (Sharon explained the difference to me). There were three fancy armchairs and a grand piano. A mess of trinkets were scattered around the edges – along walls and in front of large, latticed windows, so there was still room enough to have a tennis court. Well, maybe, I exaggerated a little bit, but that living room could store a few acres of corn.

There was a smaller room in the back – the TV room, Sharon told me. I snuck a peek during the that time when I was ignored by one and all. The TV was bigger than we had ta home, but there was seating for a choir. Before the TV went in, it was some kind of library. I could tell by the books on those shelves that they was older than dirt. (I bet the resale value of them things coulda paid my taxes for a pile of years.)

Off to the side, was a pair of huge, swinging doors, black and frightening.

"The dinning room is in there," Sharon said, seeing I was very curious.

"You eat in there?"

"Not until next year when I move into the house. I eat at the dorm. We will both be eating there tomorrow. That's where the banquet will be."

Did I mention the fireplace? I coulda put the bed from Sharon's room in there and slept on it. Actually, lighting a fire was against college, state, federal and UN regulations, just as well, 'cuz there weren't enough trees in the state to keep that thing in firewood. Instead, they parked a huge Russian tea pot in front of it on a table with cups, saucers, spoons, sugar, cream and I don't know what all.

"One of the sisters from years ago came from Russia," Sharon explained. "She donated this a few years ago. It sure beats Mom's kettle, don' it?"

Before we could claim our tea, we had to make the rounds. Sharon introduced me to the house "mother" first. She lived in a downstairs apartment and, I guess, made certain that the "sisters" behaved themselves. If she had a huge bulldog to chase away boys, I'd have been more impressed. She was a retired accountant and looked roughly eighty-years old. She was friendly enough and didn't treat me like some hobo fresh from the tracks.

Then I was introduced to the sorority president and her father. She wasn't very pretty, and her father owned a high-hat hotel in the state capital.

He was the first. I met three lawyers, a big company executive, a business owner, three business executives, a bank president, and an appellate judge. The closest thing to a working man I met was a horse doctor. At least I could talk with him and not feel like a circus clown.

The tea was spicy. I don't like tea, but this stuff was pretty good. It needed only a pinch of sugar. I even asked for a second cup. Drinking from one of them fancy cups while holding onto the saucer was galling. I wanted to carry the cup and leave the saucer on the serving table, but I knew that wasn't done. I didn't want to embarrass my daughter. I had to remind myself – *after taking a swallow, put the cup back on the saucer*. Twice, I nearly forgot.

These were just two of the times when I felt mortified.

The worst was yet to come.

Madam President called for our attention. She welcomed the dads and reminded us that there were several activities for the following day. There was a football game in the afternoon and a concert in the evening (some rock group I never heard of before or since, so they were, likely, world famous). Between, there would be a dinner at the sorority. I and the other dads were invited.

"Between meal and dessert," she continued with a smile that was pretty scary, "we'd like each father to read an original poem for, and dedicated to, his daughter. Please, no epics. A sonnet or less will do very well."

Suffering wangdoodles! I knew I shouldn't have come. Me write a poem?! I'd rather amputate my own leg. What I knew about poems wouldn't fit in a skeeter's navel! To write something and read it before all those young women and their fathers was impossible, intolerable, impossible and intolerable! I'd rather face a firing squad. I'd rather battle a wolf barehanded. I'd rather jump in the river and drown.

If I was nervous before, I was terrified now. I was shaking. I vowed, the moment Sharon and I were alone, that she'd have to drive me back to the motel. I'd load up and drive home.

"I didn't expect that," she whispered, taking my arm.

She was smiling. Well, that was Sharon. She could force a smile no matter what the occasion, but I can't pretend. Still, with her holding me by the arm, I managed to keep a scream locked away.

College was no place for me!

Sharon could feel the heat as we left. She knew what I was thinking. She wouldn't slash my tires or hold me prisoner, but she hoped she could keep me from spoiling her weekend.

She drove me to her dormitory. She held my arm as she escorted me in. She saw me to a comfortable chair in the modest, little lobby and bade me wait for her. So, I sat, feeling an utter fool, while young women giggled and shrieked playfully and talked as they came in or went out. There was an older, matronly woman behind the counter in the lobby who eyed me suspiciously. She didn't care for the young men who loitered while waiting for someone, but she, obviously, had me pegged as a perverted old man stalking quail on a college campus. I wanted to go to the counter and push her smug expression into the back of her head. Sharon, however, would be shamed and displeased, so I endured.

Twelve unending minutes later, Sharon reappeared with a small, attractive girl. She was pretty – very pretty, but she barely came up to Sharon's shoulder. She looked like a twelve-year old, but her smile was warm enough to melt a field of snow.

"Melanie, may I introduce my father," Sharon began as if she were one of them royal ladies we see in movies. "Father, this is Melanie ________, my roommate."

I don't remember the last name. It sounded foreign.

"Sharon talks about you often," the little girl announced. "I'm happy to meet you."

"I'm going to show Papa around campus," Sharon said. "I invited Melanie to come with us."

"I'm sorry," she said. "I'm trying to catch up on my history and lit. I'm so far behind, I promised I'd use the weekend to finish my reading."

I didn't know what to say, so I didn't say nothing.

"I'm glad to meet you," the girl continued. "Sharon is a great roommate. She tells me great stories about the farm. I've never been on a farm."

"I promised I'd bring her home some weekend," Sharon told me.

"You will be welcome," I said, to be polite.

Young girls make me nervous, but Sharon and Becky would treat Melanie as an honored guest. I'd probably avoid seeing her except at mealtimes. Still, if she was Sharon's friend, she'd want for nothing.

Sharon had a hand full of recipe cards and a pen.

"I know you don't have paper and pen," she said.

I accepted these items with confusion.

"To write your poem," she smiled.

I know she wanted to make me feel better, but she made me feel worse.

"Shar, I can't do this – this – I can't do it."

"That's because you think poetry is a pile of long words and lots of rhyming."

"Well, ain't it?"

She smiled. She wanted to laugh, but Sharon knew that would make me feel small.

Sharon had a parking sticker for the dorm, but she didn't have a campus sticker. We had to walk from the dorm to the college. She showed me where her classes were. We even went into a couple buildings and peeked into the empty classrooms. They didn't look much.

She took me to the bookstore and the capital building – or whatever it was. It had a name, but, to me, it looked a little like the state capitol in miniature. Inside was a ballroom, a huge and fancy lobby, a big cafeteria, and a bowling alley underneath (we didn't go there). She bought me a coffee and a iced tea for herself. We went to one of the hundred or so tables and sat to chat.

"Papa, I've lived eighteen years in the farm world," she said. "Now, I live in a college world. They aren't two worlds, Papa. It's just that my farm world has gotten bigger."

I eyed her carefully. What she said made sense, but – she put it strangely. She knew how I felt. She smiled.

"That's a poem, Papa: One world growing enough to include another. Not very clever, and no big, long words, and, I don't think, a single rhyme, but it's my feeling, and my words, so it's my poem. Understand?"

She was daring me. All those times I dared her on the farm to do something she really didn't want to do – those were dares. Now, she was throwing it back in my face.

"I'm glad I got to meet your roommate," I said. "She's very pretty – prettier than you, if I had my hand on a Bible and yer mother wasn't around, but you're my daughter. You're beautiful."

She smiled large.

"You see? You're a poet! That's why you needn't worry about this silly dinner thing. I'm proud of you, Papa. I want you there. If you run away, I'll be very hurt."

That sure put a different light on it!

She pushed the pen and little stack of recipe cards across the table to my side.

"Just a few words, Papa. One side of the card only, and you don't have to use all the space. Just a little message, from you to me. It don't need to be fancy or brilliant. Oh, and you won't get counted off for spelling."

Well, I was still going to make a fool of myself, but it was, suddenly, bearable.

I spent the night staring at blank recipe cards. I paged through Gideon hoping for – I don't know. Devine intervention? I tossed and turned. Every time I dropped off to sleep, I saw blank recipe cards. I saw all them fancy-Dan dads laughing at me and calling me names. I managed to catch thirty minutes or so before Sharon came around and pounded on my door.

"Let me take you to a great place for breakfast," she smiled as only Sharon can smile. "Of course, you'll have to pay."

"Ain't hungry," I said.

"Then, I'll pay at a terrible place to have breakfast."

How could she be so cheerful on the day of my execution?

"Let me shave and get dressed first," I said, weary and grouchy.

"Did you write your poem?"

I grumbled. Still, she wouldn't grouch. She didn't even scold. This made me feel even worse.

She took me around campus for a more complete tour. The place was nearly deserted because most everyone was at the game. We could hear the crowd noise wherever we were, but Sharon never understood football, and I never cared for it.

She took me to the library. I was amazed. There were three floors. They was all crammed with books. I never saw so many books. There were books on things I never heard of afore, and they was books in, I don't know, how many languages.

"Got any poetry books in here?"

"Ah, no, Papa," she said. "I won't let you steal. Besides, it won't sound right."

"What?"

"You reading Longfellow or Shakespeare – it wouldn't sound like you. You're a man of the soil, Papa. Reading a translation of Hesoid wouldn't do, either. It would sound _______."

She used a word here I ain't never heard afore.

"Soak it all up, Papa," she suggested.

She was gone for a minute and returned with a small scrap of paper and a pencil. The paper was for student notes; there was printing on the back. The pencil was that kind you see golfers carrying around, short and no eraser on the end. Sharon sat me down at an empty desk with six chairs around it.

"I'm going to freshen up, Papa. Write something, even if it's wrong."

Out of nowhere, I recalled our first conversation.

"You ain't a good idea."

I started with that thought and went through six lines and, maybe, forty words. It was crap, but the words said what I wanted Sharon to know. How she felt about them – well, she'd just have to put up with being embarrassed and, maybe, laughed at. She'd get over it, and I would be out of town, never to be seen or heard again.

The "banquet" was early, so dads and daughters could change and go to the concert. Sharon and I weren't going to the concert. I wanted to get on the road before it got too dark. I planned to go to church with Sharon the following morning, but I'd save on the hotel and – well, there was a good chance that I'd embarrass Sharon so much that she sooner not see me again for a while.

Well, we finished eating. It was a very good meal – well, not near as good as Becky's, but it was first class. I didn't eat much. I tried, but my stomach was in a knot. I was afraid I'd spit up if I ate much. The girl and dad across from us at table chatted like myna birds. Sharon tried to talk to me. So did the dad sitting across from me, but I just couldn't talk. I, for certain, couldn't "chat."

There was a head table and two others, just as long, on either end. When the sorority girls ate of an evening, they sat on only one side so everybody could see everybody else. Because the dads was there, both sides of the tables was used. I was happy to have my back to most of the room. It was bad enough to be gawked at by those I could see.

Four girls, whose fathers couldn't (or wouldn't) come, were made to wait table. They wore fancy aprons and brought us our blue-plates and took them away after we finished. They disappeared behind double swinging doors to wait for the humiliation to cease before bringing out our dessert plates.

Madam President began by announcing the gallows were open. She insisted her father begin the torture, probably, because she knew he would outshine the rest of us peons. Well, he stood and rattled off a gem. It took all of half a minute, but – I thought this would be an excellent time to die.

The death march went down one table and back up and around and the lawyers and bankers were rippin' and rhymin' and personifyin' and symbolizin' and I don't know what all until I knew my scribbled lines were worse than bringing up what little supper I managed to get down.

Finally, it was my turn. I vowed to die brave.

I stood on wobbly legs and spoke with a trembling voice while holding the library scrap paper in my shaking hands. I didn't bellow. But I was bold. After a few more minutes, I'd never see any of these big shots again.

When I finished, there was polite applause as there had been for all the others. I crumpled the paper in my hand and sat down before I fainted. The room spun around, and my vision went dark – but only for a second. I felt Sharon pry the paper out of my hand.

Thank God! It was away. It would go into the trash. I was gonna spend the next hundred years tryin' to bury this horrible memory.

Now, Sharon never does get to use any of that fancy English learnin' and readin'. She comes home and gets married to a local boy – a good, hard-working, level-headed boy who went to college for only a year. I never heard Sharon lord it over him because she was a college graduate with the framed document to prove it. Well, she wasn't that kind. When Becky and me decided we'd had about all the fun we could stand, we "sold" the farm to Sharon and Gil for a song. We moved into town, near the square. Sharon worked for Lawyer Thompson. He didn't give a rat's ass that Sharon didn't know no law or any such, he wanted her because she was smart as a whip and learns faster than lightnin' (his words). Becky and me was so proud. Lawyer Thompson served two terms in the state senate before he had all the fun *he* could stand. He came back to practice law in his home county.

Wednesdays was the highlight of my week. I'd go to Lawyer Thompson's office and take my girl out to lunch (Becky treated her on Fridays). Well, I walk in and find Lawyer Thompson at the front counter examining the morning mail.

"Hey, you un-convicted fraud!" he says to me. "I sent Sharon to the bank with the morning's graft. She won't be a tick. Go back and have a sit down."

Lawyer Thompson is always talking to the locals that way, and he's always talkin' about bilking people outta their life savings, but that was hogwash. If you had to appear in court, Thompson was the man you wanted on your side. Very few of his clients were ever fined and none done jail time. He knew contract law and helped me out twice. He once defended a pauper's family from a frivolous state lawsuit, won the case, and never got a nickel for it. He weren't no superman and had no superpowers, but he'd go the mat for a client. There ain't a more respected man in the county and our Sharon is his right-hand man.

Well, I did what he said. I went to Becky's desk and had a sit down. A moment later, Lawyer Thompson walked rapidly past me on his way to the office.

"Don't steal the brick-a-brack," he warned.

I leaned back in Sharon's chair. I'd love to have one like it. If I hinted hard enough, she might buy me one for Christmas, but that would be taking advantage.

To my left was the typewriter she used. All she had to do was swivel her chair and the light from the window would be at her back while she typed. To my front was a desk with files and file folders to the upper left and mail – incoming and outgoing – on the upper right.

Sharon had only four personal items on her desk. There was a small, framed wedding picture of her and Gil. Over her desk was a thick and heavy slab of glass. Under it was a list of important phone numbers and addresses and a small, current calendar.

Toward the lower left of the glass was a picture of her son. She'd named him after the brother she never knew. It was an older picture. My grandson had enough teeth to smile with, but his stubby little legs were those of a toddler. The second picture was of baby Esther, named after Gil's favorite granny. Old enough to walk and create havoc in real life, the photo was of her at the age of three days, still wrapped in the hospital blanket.

On the lower right side, under the glass, was a small scrap of paper with faded pencil scribbles on it. It was all smoothed out, now, and in a spot where she was certain to see it every day. It was the paper she pried out of my hand at college all them years afore.

Mark Williams

The Bowl of Red Cherries

I am to international travel what a mime is to radio (stolen from somewhere), but I joined the Army specifically to get free fare to Germany. Unlike many of my contemporaries, I wasn't what Bob Newhart called a "griper." Viet Nam closed out and I was in the peace-time Army as an infantryman – a "ground pounder." I didn't mind playing in the dirt, taking my turn on guard duty, standing CQ (I'd get the following day "off"), or polishing equipment to be ready for the next inspection. I was in Europe and getting paid for the honor.

It was over a year before I realized there was somewhere other than Heidelberg to spend a weekend. Unlike most in my unit, I didn't drink my pay. I opened an account and took full advantage of the German rail system and the community bank. I was building up quite a pile for an enlisted man.

American Express tours were always advertised. Many of them were slated for long weekends (Washington's Birthday, Thanksgiving, the Fourth, etc.). After I built up leave time, I could spend a day or two (or three) and book a tour for a very nice price.

I went to Tunisia just to visit Carthage (we spent, maybe, and hour there). I was disappointed, but not too much. I saw and experienced many things I found interesting. My roommate (an Air Force officer), spoke French, and made me privy to many things I would have otherwise missed.

I did two days in Rome and two in Athens over a long weekend. It was during the winter months and cold, but I got to see where Audrey Hepburn sat on the Spanish Steps in *Roman Holiday* and the more frequented tourist venues. Moreover, I got the Greek "disease." I didn't care much for the country, the food, the history, or the culture when our plane touched down, but I returned a Greek fanatic. I bought a pocketbook of (ancient) Greek plays at the airport on our way out. I read it from cover to cover (I have it still). I enrolled in a correspondence class in Ancient Greek history, took three more classes in graduate school (years later), and even introduced the Greek motif in a community theater play I directed (years and years later).

Okay. Whoopie! I took trips while most of the other troops were either reminiscing over their latest drunk or looking forward to their next one. Well, I suffered, too. Oh, how I suffered!

I do not get air sick; I get sinus pain! Whenever I flew, I knew I was in for a vicious headache and a rebellious stomach. Fortunately, I outgrew this malady, but during my Army years my head and stomach punished me severely. I knew I was in for anguish whenever I signed up for a tour, but I signed up anyway. I was willing to make the sacrifice.

When I saw an advert for a flight to Israel, I didn't give it a thought. I sacrificed both a week's leave, my head, and my stomach for this opportunity. I saw Masada, the Dead Sea, Bethlehem, Nazareth, the "Sea" of Galilee, Capernaum, etc., etc., *and* etc.

Two episodes stand out.

After a guided tour through the streets of Jerusalem, we were encouraged to have a look and/or a shop before meeting back at the bus thirty minutes later.

I wasn't brave, mind you, merely stupid. On purpose, I guided my feet toward a Palestinian area – always looking for that curio to send home. I'd, previously, bought a box of Jaffa oranges which the seller shipped home to my folks. I think that put me back eleven dollars. *Dollars*, mind you. Israel was in the grip of a de-riculous inflation crisis. If you had hard currency, you could buy nearly anything for a song. West German marks and American dollars were the nearest things to pure gold. The locals paid for many things with telephone tokens. It was the only Israeli currency with a set value. Twenty shillings in the morning might be worth only sixteen shillings by nightfall. A phone token, however, had a set value, i.e.: one phone call.

Of course, I bought some local money. It was the only souvenir I could keep since I was rationed to a wall locker and a footlocker in the billets, and both were subjected to periodic inspections – no room for oil lamps or wall plaques.

I passed by a Palestinian bakery. I don't recall seeing any bread, but I did see some confections that looked both strange and alluring. I ducked inside to find a young man in his early twenties behind the counter. I pointed to three items which he scarfed up and put in a paper bag. I asked "how much" in German. I know everyone speaks English, but I was in a Palestinian area where Jews and Americans are seldom venerated.

The shopkeeper gave me a number. I thought it was pretty damned high, but I refused to make a fuss. I pulled out a large, Israeli bill and handed it over. He could tell the amount by the color. He said something, took the bill and vacated the shop in one quick hurry.

Here is a conundrum!

A Palestinian had fled his own shop. My clothes marked me as an American. My haircut marked me as a military person. Did the shop attendant leave to gather up his buddies? Was the shop filled with explosives? Had he gone away to initiate an ambush? Was some thug going to come through the door with a huge cutlass and carve me up into bite-sized morsels?

This would be a very good time to take my bag and vacate the area!

Because I sensed no immediate danger, I hesitated. If I left now, someone might accuse me of looting the shop. I didn't feel too good. I may have said a quick "Our Father," or I may have reflected upon how very stupid and careless I was.

For, seemingly, hours, I was – for all practical purposes – the owner of a small bakery. My primary concern, strangely, was that someone, some *legitimate* someone would come in to purchase a loaf of bread – or, maybe, two. There I'd be, with my teeth in my mouth, completely unable to attend the shopper or even understand what he or she wanted. I knew no Hebrew, no Arabic, and precious little German. Strangely, this was the predicament that most frightened me.

Ten or twelve hours later (it couldn't have been more than five minutes), the young man returned clutching a handful of bills. He'd asked for a few cents (or their equivalent) and I'd thrust a hundred dollars (or the local equivalent) at him. I suspect, though I didn't investigate, that the young man had rushed off to a nearby Jewish establishment to break that huge bill.

I thanked the man profusely in two languages. We were both smiling when I left.

My faith in humanity got a big boost that day!

However, patient reader, the primary memory of my trip to Israel occurred on my first morning. We were bussed to a Jerusalem hotel. Somehow, I was assigned a single room. That was propitious. I knew I would probably be driving the porcelain bus that night, and I preferred doing so in private. My head was throbbing, and I declined an invitation to the blue-plate at the hotel.

I woke up with the Mighty Joe Young of headaches and a stomach in spin cycle. I staggered into the bathroom and pulled out my safety razor. The noise of coaxing lather out of an aerosol can, and the thunder of scraping my face with a new blade, were tumultuous. My head gradually returned to health, but my stomach remained in rebellion.

I needed something to settle my tummy. If I could have a few strawberries or a banana, I'd have a fighting chance. I took the steps. I feared the elevator might bring on an unwanted performance.

It was early. The staff was in the process of setting up the breakfast buffet. Yogurt, I decided; a fruit yogurt would be just the ticket. Fresh fruit: grapes, grapes my kingdom for some grapes! Alas, I had no kingdom.

I saw fish. Boiled fish, broiled fish, salted fish, raw fish – it hurt my stomach just to look on it. There were eggs, hard boiled. There was an array of everything I couldn't *stomach*.

Then –

In the middle of the table. In a large salad bowl. In a *very* large salad bowl! Soaking in delicious juice, I spied the reddest, ripest, most succulent cherries I'd ever seen! I tasted them ten feet away.

I grabbed a cereal bowl with one hand and the serving spoon with the other. I filled that bowl. It took five goes to fill it up. I grabbed a spoon and retired to a small table to enjoy the feast that would save my life. I got two of those perfect, red, ripe, delicious cherries and a nice helping of juice on that glittering, silver implement. With the greatest anticipation, I opened my mouth to admit nature's medicine where it would work magic.

OLIVES!

I suppose I could have expressed my disappointment by emptying my stomach over the table, but there wasn't anything to empty. I realized that I, the champion American goon, was sitting behind a bowl of olives for all and sundry to laugh at. Quickly, before the staff returned with more inedible food, I moved to another table far away from the crime scene.

One young woman passed me twice while fulfilling her duties. I was sitting near the swinging doors leading to the kitchen. I was, I'm sure, looking as lost and forlorn as a frightened puppy. On her next trip to the kitchen, she paused.

"May I get you something, sir?"

She spoke in English. Clothes and haircuts are dead giveaways.

"Do you have cream of wheat?"

"Sugar and cream?"

"Straight up!"

She disappeared. Minutes later, she set down a bowl of goop before me. She even brought me a spoon.

She may not have saved my life, but she was, to me, the Lady with the Lamp.

Before returning to my room (feeling so much better), I thanked her profusely. The thought of asking on my own behalf never entered my head. Thankfully, a sister of mercy came to my rescue. I will bet a bowl of cherries she knew who left those olives on an otherwise vacant table.

Crazy Americans!

A Matter of Principle

For nearly two decades, I'd been knocking around from one radio station to the next. Most stations have mostly syndicated yack-yack programs that allow for twelve to fifteen minutes of local advertising an hour with negligible production costs. However, stations are required to air so much local content per week. Enter *moi*, Grant Cobb, local feature producer, director, editor and on-air talent. Note: Rule number one in local radio: keep employees to the absolute minimum.

I've interviewed local florists, local hobbyists, local celebrities, local politicos, local housewives, local businessmen, local police officers, local eccentrics, and local whatever else.

Once in a hundred programs, it's interesting.

Over the years, I've become pretty good at what I do. When the program director begins leaning on me to do something specific to placate the owner, or his wife, or (on one occasion) his girlfriend, I type out my resignation. My philosophy is, if I do all the production work, *I* and only *I* decide what *I* do. It may seem as if I'm shooting myself in the foot, but you would be amazed at how many stations want my services. I, always, step into a new job at higher pay. Being nominated for three awards helps. I plan on get a big cash infusion when I *do* win an award.

Currently, I'm in Resume Speed, Kansas. One might think I'd reached the end of the line, but I view it as one more port-of-call. I don't mind small towns. In fact, I prefer them.

Quite by accident, as I'm working on a feature, someone mentions "some guy from California" he met in the local hardware store.

"I happened to mention I was refurbishing an outbuilding," says the local patron.

"This guy from California asks me about it. He's interested. He even came home with me to look over the project. He had some good suggestions and ideas. He claims he built his own house back in California – all except the wiring and plumbing."

Nearing the end of my current project, my ears perked up.

"What's the guy's name," I asked, thinking I could meet him and have a chat.

"Perry Whitworth."

"I'd like to meet him," I said.

He invited me out to his farm the following afternoon.

I spent the morning editing my material and punching out my "voice over." (Please, don't ask why I use TV terminology. It's a bad habit I picked up as a novice.)

Perry Whitworth!

It can't possibly be *the* Perry Whitworth. Still, hope springs eternal.

As a big fan of radio, back in the day when it was entertaining, Perry Whitworth could be heard three or four times a week. As a collector of old shows, I knew him as the voice of Darth Vader, or the 1930's version of Darth Vader. The serial was *Tommy Stone: Super Spy.*

It was sponsored by a wheat cereal that, along with the program, was aimed at young people. Perry's voice was heard only every third or fourth episode over a super-secret radio. He'd taunt Tommy Stone, always hot on the trail, but who could capture only the villain's henchman. The fifteen-minute serial aired weekdays for three years. The concluding episode, culminated in the capture of Perry Whitworth's alter ego.

Perry's distinctive voice was made for radio. He could be syrupy soothing, a sinister crime boss, or a bullying oaf. In my audio collection, he appeared on *Gunsmoke*, once as a busybody, old coot, and twice as a gunman: the first time, William Conrad guns him down, and the second time, he's run out of Dodge.

Perry, also, appeared in detective shows, theater and movie take-offs, variety shows, and comedies. He became a regular on three popular comedy shows that ran concurrently. He was a cranky neighbor in one, a pompous politician in another, and a supercilious bully of a boss in the third. His trademark in the latter was his propensity for getting tongue-tied and reciting hilarious monologues. Of course, the writers created the monologues, but Perry read them so rapidly and emphatically that he fetched many a belly-laugh from studio audiences.

He made the jump to TV in the early days, appearing with Burns and Allen among others.

There was a time when millions of people knew the name Perry Whitworth. I didn't know him from either radio or TV (I'm not old enough), but Old-Time Radio is my hobby and I have collected many cassettes of the classics.

It couldn't be *the* Perry Whitworth. In Kansas? How do you get 'em out on the farm after they've seen Hollywood?

I went out to the building project knowing it was a waste of time. However, if it was Perry Whitworth, and I didn't chase him down, I'd fire myself.

He was, indeed, *the* Perry Whitworth.

I recognized him by his expansive form. He's six five, if an inch, but he is generously proportioned around the middle. His moustache is exactly as it appeared in his publicity stills, though it was white now rather than black. He was wrestling some lumber through a rip saw when I drove up. The local man who tipped me off (I'm ashamed to admit I forgot his name), introduced us.

"I got interested in carpentry and woodworking when I was a teenager," he informed me. "When I made enough money in radio, I resumed the hobby. Eventually, I hung out a sign and began working commercially."

"When did you find the time?" I asked, recalling his copious radio work.

"Weekends, mostly, and the off-season when most of the shows had summer replacements."

He was polite, but he was more interested in completing his task than talking about the old days. He did agree to meet me for breakfast the following morning.

I selected the best breakfast venue in town. It was a far cry from any posh L.A. feed bag, but people came from far and wide to eat at the Silver Plow. I expected the name would keep Perry Whitworth away. Little did I know, he was a country boy of sorts. The house he built for his wife was two hours away from the radio and television studios.

"If you don't know exactly where our place is, you'll never find it," he boasted.

Perry liked to "lunch" with writers and engineers, mostly. He was comfortable with them and forged many lasting friendships.

"Bill Conrad and I used to go out for a drink or two after work, sometimes," he announced. "I used to hang around with John Dehner. I met him when we were recording *Gunsmoke*, but we didn't get close until he was working as an animator for Disney."

"You seem the kind of guy who makes friends easily," I said, hoping to egg him on.

"I suppose," he mused. "Mostly, I was interested in the technical side of things. I had more good friends in the crew than I did among the actors. Marion and Jim Jordan used to come out to our place two or three times a year and spend the night two – just to get away. That was always fun."

I'll bet.

There was one facet of this little-known if ubiquitous radio star. He weighed two-hundred pounds which, back in the day, was gargantuan. He was thirty-six years old when Pearl Harbor was hit and in high demand. He wasn't tied to any one series. Freelancing fetched relatively paltry sums. However, in any given week, Perry Whitworth was making as much as any of the radio "stars." When the young men were called up, they went to war. Dennis Day did a stint in the Navy, Jimmy Stewart flew bombers over Europe, Clark Gable was, also, in the Air Corps though he, apparently, was largely a PR airman. Phil Harris, even, went into the Merchant Marine with part, or all, his band. At his age and weight, Perry was a walking draft deferment.

Perry Whitworth, however, wanted to contribute. He was not a fighter and, certainly, no hater. However, he couldn't abide living the high life while so many young men were suffering hardship and death. He and his wife, June, discussed the issue frequently until Perry considered himself a shirker. With the aid of his devoted wife and extraordinary determination, Perry shed thirty pounds and enlisted in the Navy.

He and June had a healthy stash to see her through the duration, but she took a job in a shipyard churning out Liberty Ships. She wasn't very good at secretarial work, so they put her out with the "women's squad." These venturesome women, some motivated by patriotism and some in need of cash while their men were off to war, were taught skills and took up the slack whenever and however they could. June learned how to weld and do basic wiring.

Perry, or "Gramps" did his best to keep up with the kids. Much of the physical training was too taxing, and he was constantly lagging – except in swimming. He wasn't much of a swimmer, but he could float for days had the need arose. Additionally, the youngsters made fun of him, a "big Hollywood big-shot" who couldn't sing, dance, tell jokes (*sans* writers), or play an instrument. However, Perry had the voice of a grizzled old Chief Petty Officer. He bellowed orders in the middle of the night and had his fellow "'cruits" forming a bucket brigade for a fire that never was. The officers were not amused. Perry spent a night in the brig and two-weeks of "extra duty."

The incident, however, proved a boon to his military career. If there is one quality both sailors and leadership responded to in war, it was a manly voice bellowing orders. Perry was eased into leadership positions – exceedingly minor, of course, but he was earmarked for better things.

He was sent to gunnery school. By the time he earned his first stripe, he was a gunner's mate. Upon completion of advanced training, he was given another stripe and kept as an assistant instructor. Soon, he was habitually granted passes to rehearse and perform in radio shows. He and June frequently enjoyed a Sunday together and, over time, entire weekends.

I was getting a lot of information. Perhaps, you expect me to take notes. Had I any integrity, I would have. However, my competitors in "the business" don't bother with accuracy; they chow down on talking points and submit their "stories" after running them through the propaganda mill. Listening to Perry Whitworth, I didn't give a damn about anything other than his ability to entertain me. I have no axes to grind. My story, when I punch it out, will be judged on "likability."

Perry was promoted again and made a gunnery instructor. If he requested, the Navy tried to keep Perry's evenings free so he could leave base, rehearse for an hour (or less), do a live broadcast, and report back to base before midnight. Several times, he missed his deadline, but his punishments, if any, were mild.

"I was satisfied," he announced. "I wanted to do my bit. Training gunners was a valuable service. Then, the Navy caught Victory Fever. The brass wanted to throw everything we had to finish off the enemy quickly. I got orders for sea duty."

He puffed out his cheeks.

"Seasick?"

"Not half," he replied.

"So, you were hustled off to Tokyo," I surmised.

He laughed.

"Remember, young man, I was in the Navy. Because I lived, practically, on the Pacific Ocean, they sent me to Virginia. That made sense to someone."

"See any action?"

"Have you heard about that group the captured the U-boat?"

I whistled.

"You were in on that?"

Perry Whitworth laughed. It wasn't the laugh he used on any of his radio programs. This one was playful without the hint of his trademark, sardonic lilt.

"I was over three hundred miles away," he reported. "I was on a destroyer in another group doing the same job: anti-submarine work."

"Get any?"

"The Germans were running out of subs. The pilots strafed and bombed, but whales and shadows, mainly. They did get one sub. By the time we got there, the crew was in the water and the sub was down by the stern. I commanded a twenty-millimeter mount. We were supposed to be anti-aircraft, but the only aircraft we ever saw were ours. I had the crew fire off a few rounds. We even got a few hits, but – so what? No one was aboard and the sub was finished anyway."

I didn't say anything. I didn't feel obligated.

"We went around and rescued part of the crew. We off-loaded them to the escort carrier where they reunited with other survivors. I never saw a sorrier bunch of boys. They were really scraping the bottom of the barrel."

He looked at me and winked.

"Look who's talking."

"I'd hardly call you the bottom of the barrel," I replied.

He shrugged.

"Regardless, that was my personal contribution to the war effort. I like to think that the kids I trained got in the licks that counted. There's no way to know, but – well, there it is."

Indeed.

There was only one thing I had to know.

"What brings you to Kansas?"

He chuckled.

"A cousin of mine, a confirmed bachelor, opened a savings account for our kids. Hell, I hardly knew the guy, but he knew me, from the radio, I guess. Anyway, June gets a call from a debt-collector agency. The bank used them to track us down. They had a dead account on their hands and wanted to clean up their books. So, I drove out here to tidy things. I've got a certified check I'm taking home. June will make sure it gets where it needs to go."

"You never did TV."

It wasn't a question. It was an observation.

"A few shows," he confessed. "I did the same characters I played on radio, but it wasn't the same. The featured players were stuck, but I was never a featured player; I didn't have a career to protect. June and I decided to turn our ranch retreat into a commercial enterprise. We never made the big bucks, but I'd never made big bucks in radio. We invested enough to keep us going in retirement."

I was impressed. I got a good story, but I wasn't certain my employer would be enthused about it. To be fair, not many listeners would appreciate it.

"Well," I sighed. "You went to war and got a couple licks in. I guess that felt rewarding."

He stopped what he was doing.

"Let me walk you back to your car," he volunteered.

That struck me as odd but hardly suspicious.

"I'm glad I went to war," he admitted. "I'd have been miserable had I not. Helping to save the crew of a defunct U-boat was *not* the contribution I'm most proud of."

He had no writers handy. Ending a sentence with a preposition was so – well, so *human*. In that instant, I considered him a friend.

"The kids on that U-boat weren't the only kids out there," he announced. "The crew of our destroyer was mostly kids. Even the petty officers, me excluded, were under thirty. Practically, the entire crew was never more than a few miles away from home before Pearl. Those kids were ready to do what the skipper demanded, but they were more homesick than scared. I was everybody's grandpa. I'd been a radio performer, and everyone knew it. They were all the time asking me about Ingrid and Betty and Joan and the other big film actresses. Hell! I didn't know any of those big movie stars, but they assumed I did.

"Finally, I gave in to their pestering. I would relate real life anecdotes of things that happened to real people, but I changed the names. I remember telling one story that happened to June. Well, nobody knew June, so I said it happened to Hedy Lamar. Pretty soon, I was changing names to fit whichever star was the pin-up-of-the-day."

"They believed you?"

"I cannot answer that. The important thing was that these boys missed their homes and families. However, they all resided in the mythical city of Hollywood. Any fairy tale I told them about that magic place was good medicine – and a morale boost. I was lying my ass off, but I enjoyed the hell out of it. However, I'm not lying when I tell you that the greatest thrill I ever got in show business was playing to audiences of five or fewer onboard that destroyer."

Random Remembering

In Germany, I was a "local hire," the lowest life form on earth. I wanted to return to Germany after obtaining my graduate degree. I'd served over three years of my Army "career" in Germany and was eager to return. Had I known . . .

I filled in government forms out the kazoo. After several months in limbo, working for a wholesaler as a delivery driver and small goods schlepper, I got a call. Would I be interested in a half-time position at a nearby high school?

No!

However, I was not in a position to refuse.

A government employee, be he a soldier or an ambassador, works only part time. Half of any government job is filling out tons of forms. If you want to wash your hands: fill out form XYZ. If you expect toilet paper to be in the men's room: fill out form XYZ, subsections 6,8 and 40. Not to complain, but my half-time job was a quarter-time job. The remaining quarter was spent filling out papers.

I couldn't complain too much. My pay as a half-time teacher was only slightly less than my full-time teaching job in the States. Further, I could bulk up, ever so slightly, by coaching football after school.

I taught three classes in the afternoon and coached the JV football team for an additional three hours after school. The games were on Saturday which I habitually reserved for "knocking about" the German environs in search of Roman remains and quaint, rural villages. Well, not when there was a game.

The following year, I was invited back – half time. Had I suspected, I'd have been looking for other employment. However, I hadn't suspected and was trapped.

After three weeks, the principal took me aside and asked if I'd be willing to teach full time. I resisted the urge to shake him by the lapels.

"I'd be amenable," I replied softly.

"Plan on it, then."

Planning and being employed by the United States Government are mutually exclusive. However, I was "promoted" at the end of the first quarter. This gave me PX privileges, access to the community bank, a ration card (coffee, booze and cigs, primarily), and a library card at the base library. This last was the jewel. I drank German coffee and eschewed both alcohol and smokes. Had I been employed a decade or so earlier, I'd have made a bundle selling ration points. Well, full-time pay was great. In addition, I could carry over my time in the Forest Service and the Army for retirement points.

Some years later, my principal (not the same one) caught me in the stairwell one morning.

"Would you like to go to G________?"

I assumed she was referring to some workshop. I'd get transportation and per diem.

"Sure," I replied, ever eager to use a government boondoggle to my own advantage.

"I looked it up," she continued. "G_______ is fifty-two miles away. If you go, you're entitled to a housing allowance."

The penny dropped!

The "prince" had "lost a slot" due to declining enrollment. G_______ had picked up a slot. If I agreed to transfer, I'd get all the perks of a State-side hire. The housing allowance would be most welcome. It was tantamount to being paid twice for the same job!

Unfortunately, G_______ was Stalag Luft X without the guard towers. Every day was an adventure. The kids ran the school while the teachers spent most of the day keeping our heads down and out of the line of fire. I did what I could to teach World History and English, but there were many days when my previous job (*sans* housing allowance) looked damned good. While in the Army, it was a truism that the best outfit was either the one you just came from, or the one to which you were reassigned. I guarantee, G_______ was *not* on either list among those of us who taught there during a very turbulent period.

I plodded on for – however long I plodded on. Gradually, the atmosphere began to stabilize. The new community commander was no-nonsense. He disciplined those soldiers whose children were under little or no discipline at home. He went so far as to transfer people out of the command which adversely impacted their promotion opportunities. Moreover, he sent people back to the States for separation from service. Likewise, a new principal was sent in and was closely monitored by the community commander. We all felt the heat and were crapping coconuts for a few months, but G_______ Junior and Senior High School began to resemble a place of learning.

World-wide, U.S. Government overseas schools were drawing down due to a reduction in the number of service personnel. The school in Panama closed, leaving the teachers and staff with the option of "retiring" or being transferred. G_______ was blessed when it gained an entire science department. Mr. and Mrs. S. tossed a coin to decide who would be department head; the advantage was additional pay; the disadvantage was additional piles of government paper.

Dave was (is) a character. He knew his science, and he had a ton of experience. He'd grown up in the Canal Zone and, save for family visits in the States, never strayed. However, he was as loony as Black Beard's parrot. Naturally, he and I bonded.

We would sit apart from the rest of the faculty at meetings because we were "discipline problems." One or the other of us could not resist launching snarky and (at times) rude comments about the top-down policies and procedures forced upon us and the unending "School Improvement Programs" (which seldom had anything to do with either school or its improvement).

Mrs. S. was the brains of the outfit. She, in the parlance of we mere mortals, "knew her stuff." Once, in the faculty lounge over lunch, I asked about a certain element. Mrs. S. looked up and to her right causing David, seated beside me, to burst into laughter.

"She's looking at the periodic table in her head," he explained.

Science and I never played well together. I memorized the abbreviations (Pb, Fe, O, etc.) but anything beyond that was Greek to me. Still, I remain curious. I was never afraid to ask Mr. and Mrs. S. about capricious concerns for no reason other than I wanted to know. Most of my concerns were dispatched quickly and in terms I could understand and remember. They never mocked me. If I stumped them – a rare event – they knew exactly where to find the answers. Of course, it would all be in Einstein-speak, but they would translate the most esoteric theories and chemical reactions in terms I could understand. Similarly, if they had a question about literature or grammar, I was ever ready to be of assistance. We had quite a round-table discussion during lunch period over a short story I'd assigned a class.

Mr. and Mrs. S. had four daughters. One of these young ladies was in my AP Lit. and AP U.S. History classes. They took education seriously and, daily, monitored each girl's assignments and scholastic progress. If they stumbled over something, mater and pater would seek clarification. They were not helicopter parents, but they – as with me – wanted to learn.

Having lived in Panama for most of their lives, the family spoke Spanish to varying degrees of competency. David was the least proficient. When confronted by a soldier (or a subversive) while collecting marine samples for his biology class, David remained silent and let his co-conspirator speak for him.

"How come he ain't talkin'?" the officious, military rifle toting inquisitor asked.

"He's mute," David's friend responded.

David knew enough Spanish to understand that much. He played along.

In Germany, we had "snow days" from time to time. The girls thought this was a hoot. In Panama, they didn't have snow days. They did, however, have "unrest days," when it was not prudent to be outside. There were, so I was told, a couple scars on the exterior of their house created by bullets.

When not seeking exhibits for science class, the family would explore the "old road" created by the Spanish of the sixteenth century. Loot was shipped from Peru to the isthmus where it was off loaded and carted cross-country to Port Royal for storage and ultimate shipment to Spain. Soldiers were assigned to escort this pelf. The escorts, being soldiers, were "light fingered." Spanish Army officers, being the King's men, would, periodically search anyone they suspected of helping themselves. The penalty for stealing the king's wealth was death. Soldiers were eager *not* to be caught with anything not officially issued. As a result, certain items would be tossed into the jungle or "accidentally" dropped along the road.

David brought to school a few items he and his family discovered. I was eager to examine these Inca artifacts. Many of them were small – very small. One was a solid gold effigy of some person or Inca god. It was hardly larger than the digit of my long finger, but it was well crafted and unexpectedly detailed. I suspect, though he never told me, that the Panamanian government frowned upon such artifacts being "exported." Likely, the family remained "unaware" of how these items got into their household baggage.

David, particularly, liked to fish in the canal. On one such adventure, he and his Spanish-speaking friend were "run over" by a huge cargo ship. They spent two nights on a mosquito infested island before attracting the attention of a patrol craft. For obvious reasons, the government did not want unauthorized personnel loitering in such a major transportation artery. They read the riot act and took the ship-wreck survivors off to jail for a lengthy interrogation.

They were thankful for the rescue and suffered the official treatment and admonishment without qualms. Mrs. S. and her friend, the Spanish speaker's wife, feared they'd been widowed. After hours of anguish, the men and their wives were re-united.

"For three whole days," he announced, "we wished we were back on that island, starving, and feeding the mosquitoes."

This jewel of an anecdote was related in words and music. David, and his Spanish-speaking friend, formed a group. They wrote and performed at various venues to supplement their government pay (his friend worked for the Canal Zone before and after the handover).

The duo recorded CDs of songs they wrote and performed. These are high-quality studio products with Mrs. S. and one (or two) of the girls providing back-up vocals. David played lead guitar with his Spanish-speaking friend on bass. When they performed or recorded, they'd hire a drummer or, I think, one of the daughters was a drummer. All the sisters, including the youngest, either sang in choir or played in band.

Periodically, David brought his guitar and an amplifier to school for a bit of music to dissect frogs by. He seldom sang. He could only sing with his Spanish-speaking friend and only when using the English-Panamanian dialect that was half imitation and half made up. The family would jet to Panama during summer break and play impromptu gigs at festivals, cookouts, or anywhere people assembled. David told me that there's a bar in Ohio that plays their CDs exclusively on Wednesday nights.

A subdued David came into the faculty room earlier than usual one morning. He checked his in box and sat down across from me. Save for a trio of other teachers checking their boxes on the way to their rooms, we were alone. David sighed.

"Do you know the three most horrifying words in the English language?"

"Tell me," I insisted, not eager to participate.

I'm on strike!

As an English teacher, I was tempted to turn pedantic and reply that, technically, his sentence consisted of four words. His expression, however, told me that discretion was in order.

Apparently, David's frivolous and, often, abrupt comments had struck a nerve. If surviving a shipwreck and overnighting on a hostile island caused Mrs. S. to lower the proverbial boom, he didn't learn. When their youngest (and last) daughter was born, David came into the hospital to check on mommy.

"How do you feel?" he asked.

"I'm okay," she croaked.

"Great, I've got to get to a disc golf game."

It was Mrs. S, who related this anecdote. When next I saw David, I informed him he was a very lucky man to still be alive.

David did not divulge his latest transgression, but he could (and, likely, would) write a song about the aftermath.

"Aren't we having breakfast this morning? *I don't know; I'm on strike.* Are the girls ready for church? *I don't know, I'm on strike.* It's your turn to drive. *I'm on strike.*"

I wish I could empathize, but I tended to take the side of the wife on this one. To top disappearing during a fishing expedition and a no-visit visit in hospital, his latest *faux pas* must rate as a hall-of-famer. I never asked Mrs. S.; David never explained.

As downtrodden as he looked and sounded, my heart didn't bleed much. The family S. ran like a fine Swiss watch. Each girl knew her chores and completed them with alacrity and without complaint. Washing, ironing, dusting, sweeping, mopping, trash removal – the whole smack. Mrs. S. did the cooking and sewing; the girls *sans* David pitched in with the rest – *before* they sat down with their homework (closely monitored by – guess whom).

The girls did not get an allowance. Instead, David sat down once a year to estimate how much he'd spend for each girl during the next twelve months. He set aside the sum for them to use as they pleased. The amounts were pro-rated in accordance with their school grade levels.

"When that's gone," David announced, "It's gone. Don't ever ask me for money."

It worked. Each girl learned to manage her finances. Even the youngest, (who liked to sing opera she composed on the fly) knew that money wasn't a resource to waste.

Further, the girls learned responsibility beyond their household routine. When they went on a long car ride, and the youngest had sung herself out, the second oldest would read aloud to them. When she opted for my AP Lit class, she selected *Pride and Prejudice.* The others enjoyed these recitations. The younger one based her next few operas on this classic.

When they took a train or were off to Panama or the States during the summer recess, one of the girls was put in charge – even the youngest.

"Get us on the right train. Get us to the check-in counter. Get us through passport control. Get us to the gate. Get us on the right plane."

If the "team leader" got confused or lost, she dared not ask mater or pater. Instead, she would ask a uniformed official – and two of them could do so in German. The others learned, very quickly, that Germans unable to speak English are difficult to find – particularly at train stations and airports.

I wondered about the third daughter. I never had her in class, but I saw her frequently around school. In three years, she spoke only a single word to me.

It was after the last bell and the busses had departed. After school activities i.e., athletic practice, ROTC drill team and rifle team, band rehearsals, et al, were just gearing up. The S. family, habitually, left as a unit. Mrs. S. would drive to the elementary school and pick up the youngest girl. One of her siblings would be detailed to keep an eye on her while the others were occupied with various activities.

Whiling away my time before I was officially "released," I opted to check my box in the faculty lounge. If anyone tarried within, we might enjoy a nice chin wag while watching the clock's minute hand to set us free.

I left my classroom, in the "temporary" outbuilding (*temporary* is a government euphemism for any shoddy structure used until the end of time) and walked briskly to the nearest of the main building's entrances. Just as I reached out to pull the door open, it was pushed open (*thrown* more like) by young Stephanie.

"Hi," she said, in a voice so timid and weak as to be barely audible.

"Hello," I replied, cheerily.

That was the entire extent of her verbal exchanges with me. Her verbosity with her peers was, likewise, abbreviated. I didn't fault her for rationing her words, but expecting to join in any conversation with her was vacuous.

During the year, various student activities were arranged. One of these was a lunchtime basketball tournament. It was to be three-on-three and, at least, one of the three must be a girl. Stephanie was quickly recruited by two of the upper classmen. They could shoot baskets with amazing accuracy, but they couldn't dribble worth a pinch. Stephanie, however, could dribble upstairs and down and was not a bad shot. The trio purchased matching T-shirts and had them silkscreened: Steph and the guys.

I don't know how this team did, but I often wondered how they talked her into it. I imagine they did all the talking while Steph nodded from time to time.

During the waning days of the school's existence, a quartet of staff gathered to eat lunch in one of the science rooms. One day, I got my cafeteria tray early and made my way through the halls. Upon reaching Mrs. S.'s room, it was vacant – save for Stephanie waiting for the microwave to finish heating the lunch she'd made herself at home.

This is my chance, I thought. She must speak!

"Where's your mom?"

Stephanie looked at me and shot the storeroom door with her pistol finger. She wasn't hostile or rude, but she was, as always, silent.

During one spring break, the family booked a cruise on the Med. They were very excited about getting a crack at the sun while lounging around on a cruise ship. Of course, when they returned, I was anxious to learn of their adventures.

"There were only three bunks to a room," Mrs. S. reported. "David and I decided to give the girls a break, so we took Steph in with us."

There's a question begging to be begged. What, I wondered, was so horrible about Stephanie? She wasn't a practical joker, nor did she show signs of maliciousness.

"Stephanie," her mother reported, "never shuts up!"

"Stephanie? Your daughter, Stephanie? The Sphinx?"

"That's at school," David informed. "At home, you can't get a word in."

The last two years in G_______ were the two most satisfying years of my professional life. The days of the unsupervised penal colony were a dim, horrible memory. Students, parents, teachers, administrators, the cooks, the cleaning crew – we were a family. Any family has its problem relatives, but they were few and easily kept in line.

Since the school was closing, we teachers had first choice in reassignment. This was difficult for those who had become acclimated to Germany; all the service schools in "Dutch Land" were drawing down. I, however, was eager for a change. I put in for the two high schools on Okinawa, realizing I mightn't have enough seniority. My remaining choices were listed alphabetically since I'd go wherever the government sent me.

I got my first choice and was off to Kadena High School in the Ryukus. David and Mrs. S. were dispatched to Brussels International School. So long as they were two plane connections from Panama, they'd be happy there.

As my first school year on Okinawa was ending, I got an email from Mrs. S.

They needed a good social studies/English teacher in Brussels. If I was interested, they would lobby on my behalf.

My blood pressure experienced a burst. It would be nice to be back in Europe and in Brussels, a beautiful city where I spent many enjoyable, rubbernecking days. I was, also, flattered that they thought of me. However, I'd experienced the adventure of one move and the hassles involved in securing orders, packing out, unloading and etcetera. The prospect of two trans-world moves in two years was too daunting to contemplate.

That, I fear, was the last I heard from and of them.

Damn!

The Way Things Was

My father was a resident engineer in Warner, Oregon. He was the lead man in the survey of a highway from Warner to the Nevada border. It was a project initiated prior to the chaos of the Depression, but it was jump-started in the late fifties. It remains unfinished, since the goal was to connect Nevada to the Pacific Ocean. It is possible, but not on a single highway.

I tell everybody that my family was here for eighteen months. However, I got to finish the fourth grade, repeat the fourth grade, and finish the fifth grade before we moved away to a less arid and more salubrious climate (and a promotion and better job for my dad). I, therefore, suspect we resided here longer than eighteen months. Regardless, this little fly speck on the map was my retirement plan from the first.

As a child, Warner was a paradise. There were hills to climb, deserts to explore, guns to shoot, arrowheads to search for, dogs galore, deer meandering about the streets, and outer space to conquer (my friends and I played Space Jockey over Cowboys and Indians by a wide margin).

I went to a school with real Indians (as they were known in a less persnickety time), Hawaiians, Chinese, and Americans from all points on the map. Most of the students, however, were born and raised in and around Warner.

Much of the local lore was heavily skewed by my imagination. Moving back upon retirement, I discovered that much of my knowledge of the area existed only in my childish imagination. There remains, however, one feature embossed upon my brain that is as pristine and flawless as memories deserve. "The Slide" is a two-and-a-half-mile steep grade up the side of a prehistoric escarpment. Hardly a week goes by without my hearing some grizzly tale about a mishap on "The Slide."

"My father surveyed that," I like to announce. "I was up and down that slide in our old Studebaker when it was nothing more than a blade scratch."

It's true! Every word is pure, unadulterated fact. It is, also, true that I eschew that highway because of "The Slide." My brother and I made an excursion, recently, through the Oregon Desert to Fields and on into Nevada. The only way back was through Warner. To get to Warner, we had to go down "The Slide" – in second gear with much braking.

"This ain't the way I remember it," I noted.

"I think they dug out some parts to add a few curves," my brother responded. "It's, probably, a good idea."

Maybe. However, I doubt that many people drove that section of highway while under the influence of *spritus fermentii*. Either they don't survive it, or they don't bother to boost about it.

I spend considerable time in and around the café. The owners do quite well dispensing ice cream and snacks (locally made cookies, muffins, and cinnamon buns), but it boasts the lowest coffee prices in town, accounting for much of their cash flow. Naturally, locals linger over coffee and chat with old friends or make new ones. Current events and gossip, as expected, undergo meticulous examination. Since the establishment is on Main Street and sandwiched between the county courthouse and two banks, the café sucks in pedestrians like a vacuum. Moreover, it is a repository of local history – much of it never managed to find its way into the history books.

A case in point:

I met a man, during the early days of my return, who sat drinking coffee while waiting on his daughter to run him home. He wore a USS LEXINGTON baseball cap.

"Were you on the Lady Lex when she went down?"

"Nah," he responded. "I got off."

Later when I repeated his terse reply, I was informed by his friends and neighbors that he was an enlisted man at the time of the Coral Sea Battle. After he was fished out of the ocean, he went home to become an officer and a fighter pilot. He returned to sea and experienced more action as the war spiraled down. After the war, he brought the CAP to Warner and, later, was instrumental in bringing commercial flights into the county. Well, the CAP and the airline are fond memories.

Some swag told me that the man was, also, responsible for the airstrip at Wagontire, a wide spot in the road (now, for sale – you can get a motel, café AND the airstrip for a song.) Like other war-time facilities, the airport was paved and used only for "emergency" stops for B-25s and SBDs training in the arid wastes. However, it is designated on FAA maps as Wagontire International Airport.

It sounds like something the old man would lobby for. He was a character. However, I doubt that he ever had the suck power required to pull off that beauty.

I was enjoying a sip and chew one morning when an elderly, leather-skinned woman waddled into the café. She wasn't what I would describe as fat, but she was BIG. She looked neither right nor left. She asked for a small bottle of water.

The cold-drink display was across from the counter and impossible to miss. I expected the man at the resister would direct her thither. He didn't. Without any hesitation, he scrambled from behind the counter, opened the glass case, secured a plastic bottle of water, and rushed back to his zone. He placed the item on the counter as if he'd conjured it like some practiced wizard. He announced the price. The woman opened the hanky she carried in her left hand and carefully counted out exact change. She thanked the man and waddled out.

"Who was that?" I couldn't help asking.

"That is Little Fox," the proprietor explained. "She's Modoc, I think. Someone told me that she was related to Captain Jack, but I'm not too sure I believe it. She doesn't get into town as often as she used to."

No wonder. She had no car. When Little Fox came to town, she walked. It was far enough to be a chore for the young and spry. I couldn't believe this elderly woman could manage such a hike at her leisurely pace.

I seldom saw Little Fox in town. I was told she raised chickens and rabbits that accounted for the bulk of her diet. She would dry and grind her own corn and make her own bread. She owned a rifle. She'd kill for meat and clothing.

Judge Bob was a native of Warner who'd been on the bench for over two decades. He was no Clarence Darrow, but he knew more about state and county law than anyone. He frequented the café, though he seldom tarried.

"I found out what *en loco parentis* means," I piped up, exercising my authority as the town smart ass.

The judge looked at me expectantly. He knew better than to attempt erudition with me.

"It means, my father drives a locomotive."

He gave me a courtesy smile. Okay, so as a comedian, I'm one step removed from asphalt. However, here was the judge, the local legal sage, and my curiosity was up. The proprietor (in a small-town café, we do *not* use "barista" – that's reserved for barbarians) was busy filling his order, so he had a few extra seconds.

"Little Fox." I announced.

"What about her?"

He didn't seem the least threatened.

"She kills deer and fishes year around," I said, repeating the local rumors. "She have a license?"

"She's a Modoc," he reminded. "She's covered by treaty law."

"Up here?" I challenged.

"She's covered as far as I'm concerned. If someone accuses her of poaching, we may have to blow the dust off some old statutes, but I don't think any lawyer in these parts would take the case. They'd have to hire some city lawyer to prosecute, and I doubt any of the suit-and-tie crowd would be caught dead in this town."

"If they tried," another patron injected. "He probably *would* be caught dead."

"I'll pretend I didn't hear that, Jim," the judge replied.

"Well, no puffed-up popinjay city lawyer is gonna push Little Fox around."

"She takes what she needs," the judge reminded. "I don't think anyone is going to make a fuss."

Well, as I found out later, Little Fox was only *part* Modoc. There was a Caucasian in the woodpile.

Little Fox lived in a dilapidated former hunting lodge three or four miles out of town. She had no electricity or running water. However, she was near enough a runoff to fetch water for her simple needs. In the summer, the stream often dried up and Little Fox had to rely on deliveries. The route was off the normal route and the driver was discouraged (but never forbidden) from driving up the dirt track to drop off the large jugs.

Though her Depression-Era cabin resembled war damage and ready to collapse in a strong wind, the interior was spotless and lovingly decorated. Instead of wallpaper, Little Fox had animal skins depicting native scenes. The woman made and mixed her own paint. She'd been offered small fortunes for each of her highly ornate creations, but she was never tempted.

The skins would be easy to steal because her "home" had no door. No one ever bothered them. Her antique rifle might fetch a healthy price at gun show. It was propped up in one corner when not in use and was, similarly, left undisturbed. It was bolt action. She removed the bolt and took it with her whenever she left her "lodge" – just in case some curious kid came by. She bought bullets from other hunters, no more than a dozen at a time. She was a crack shot. If she had to shoot twice to bring something down, she cursed herself for wasting ammunition.

She cooked over an open fire, even in winter. She had battered pots and pans she'd salvaged from local dust bins or inherited through the generosity of "neighbors."

Little Fox refused to take any money from the government. She claimed it would make her subservient or a slave to the "white man." She refused to surrender to the "conquerors."

She made and sold small crafts from the residuals of whatever she caught, trapped or killed. She seldom had more than a dozen dollars at any given time. If she couldn't make payment on her summer water, she'd be carried on the books for however long it took.

She enjoyed the rodeo and watched the proceedings every September. When not spectating, she hawked her wares. Similarly, she would sit on the hillside overlooking the community pool during summer mornings. She enjoyed watching the younger children taking lessons and splashing about.

Little Fox had no enemies. She had no friends. She spoke when spoken to and readily exchanged greetings when in the proximity of others, but she was no conversationalist. Once, according to rumor, she had a "husband." Who he was or what happened to him remains a local mystery.

It was one of the Patch-work Fiddlers who provided an interesting exposition on Little Fox. He was one of our older citizens. He'd been a cow puncher, sheep herder, seasonal Forest Service employee, blacksmith, bar tender, horse trader, and successful petty larcenist over the years. He was, however, never cited nor convicted. I know this because we served one summer on the county grand jury. A record would have prohibited his sitting.

He was a celebrity of sorts, locally, that is. He was one of the best fiddlers in the state if not the nation. I won't vouch for that. I wouldn't know a great fiddler from a beginner, but he and the other Patch-work Fiddlers were a mainstay of any Fourth of July or Rodeo celebration. They played in the parades. Spence, his preferred moniker, was hired as a solo performer at square dances and private parties.

Someone, not me, made mention of Little Fox. Though it drew a chuckle from the assembly, it went over my head. Spence happened to be sitting in the swivel chair next to mine. I elbowed him gently and wanted to know what was funny about Little Fox. There wasn't time. The DA was bringing in a "witness."

Ninety minutes later, after we had done our duty for the week, I offered to buy Spence a cup of coffee. As a widower, he was in no hurry to get home, so he walked with me a block and a half to the café.

"Ya wanna know 'bout Little Fox, huh? Well, let's have a seat, cause I'm gonna tell ya the damnedest story you'll eva hear."

It was a beaut! However, Spence was so full of bull crap, he could manure a forty-acre field without breaking a sweat. True, he exaggerated several things, but the bulk of his story was verified by dozens over the next several months. Yes, I checked out his story. I kept checking until I was satisfied Spence knew his onions.

Warner was settled by Irish, Roman Catholics. They were not among the original pioneers, but they gravitated to the area in droves. Even today, the town council is dominated by the "Irish Mafia." Understand, these people do not engage in any (known) criminal activity, but they irk many citizens by refusing to move the town beyond 1953.

In the early days, however, the Irish were vehement foes of the Indians. The major cause of umbrage was not based on either skin color or lifestyle. The Irish hated anyone who wasn't Roman Catholic. You didn't have to profess the religion, or even practice it, but you couldn't own property or hold elected office if you didn't acknowledge the "true faith."

Predictably, a young Irish lad fell elbows over tea kettle with a Modoc maiden. The tribe accepted him as the girl's husband. In Warner, however, he was a "squaw man" – not a very salubrious title either for the young Irishman or those who used the term within his earshot. Being Irish, however, he was bullheaded. He'd marry his young wife in the "white-man's way" just to (symbolically) poke his tormentors in the eye. The local padre refused to perform the ceremony either on principle or because he might lose his parish had he relented. The two protestant prelates refused – they wanted nothing to do with a Papist.

New to the region was a Russian Jew. He'd fled the old country during the "troubles" of 1848 and found freedom and livelihood in the "wild west." He hunted, trapped, skinned, butchered, fished, and hired himself out as a day laborer. He spent considerable time schlepping bags of grain, seed, and sacks of wool for the railroad. His name was Abram and, curiously, his religion was never an issue among the otherwise persnickety Irish. His muscles and work ethic deflected any objections to his worship habits.

Just south of Warner, there existed a substantial lake (currently an arid wasteland). A steamboat (gambling ship) plied the waters most evenings. A few passengers booked pleasure cruises, but there was never any guarantee the boat would tie up at either end of the lake, particularly if there was serious money in the pot. Eventually, an impressive resort was built on the California side of the lake. This became the steamboat's port-of-call. Gamblers would embark there as well as day trippers.

The resort was among the myriad of establishments that employed Abram. He accumulated enough folding money to buy a boat. He was very proud of that boat. When he was free, he'd take couples out onto the lake for a modest fee. If a couple wished to be alone, he'd rent his boat for an hour or two.

Abram had a nose for money. When he heard about the problem with the squaw man and the Modoc, he set about to turn their problem into cash. As a man of brain as well as brawn, he began looking through books and asking questions.

The lake in question lay in both Oregon and California. Neither state could claim it as its own. Therefore, the water was under the jurisdiction of the Federal Government. Congress and the Coast Guard had jurisdiction. Neither Congress nor the Coast Guard maintained a presence on the lake.

In one of his books, Abram learned that the captain of a water vessel could, legally, marry passengers. It was only a matter of securing the proper documents. The Warner Court House supplied Abram with the papers. He, then, arranged a meeting with Squaw Man and Mrs. Modoc (both names are lost). For a dollar, he'd take them on a boat ride. For an additional dollar, he'd "hitch them up." For another dollar, he'd arrange transportation to and from the resort and his boat.

There was a slight hitch. The Jewish captain could join the couple in holy matrimony, but there was hardly room in the boat for the three of them. Two witnesses were required. The groom rounded up two visitors, but he gathered a crowd of dozens.

The brave captain rowed twenty feet away from the shore and performed the ceremony using a borrowed Methodist handbook while the witnesses watched and listened from terra firma.

Little Fox is that couple's granddaughter.

The Romance That Never Was

It was my first visit to Germany in over seven years. Truthfully, I went in the guise of business. However, the business was my own.

After a week in Hannover, I opted to visit friends in Berlin. We met at the airport and in the excitement of our reunion, I was invited to a posh soiree that evening. I accepted before I realized how posh it would be. It wouldn't do, for example, to go stag. My friends, exercising far more enthusiasm than wisdom, made a concerted effort to get me a date.

Blind dates – well, that is not on my agenda. After eighteen years, my wife and I agreed, amicably, to call it a day. To return to the pretense of "dating" was simply "not on," to coin a phrase. My protests gained no traction until my well-intentioned friends were unable to procure the interest of any lady acquaintances.

Perhaps, prayer does work.

Dodging one bullet, however, was hardly a blessing. I, suddenly, faced attending a society-page affair "stag" rather than "drag." Though it had been some while, I recall how many Germans frown on such arrangements. Behind that tough, Teutonic exterior lurks a perpetual suspicion that a man alone is trolling for someone's wife or mistress.

I vowed to have a miserable evening.

On the plus side, however, the fest was scheduled for the top-floor atrium of a new, nose-in-the-air hotel in the former Eastern Sector. The mayor and other dignitaries were among the invited guests. There was bound to be lots of wine and other spirits. I could exercise my elbow while pretending to be a society snoop for some national publication. With luck, someone would tempt me with some juicy gossip in the hopes that I would publish, (leaving my non-existent employer with a walloping liable suit).

It could be a win-win situation for an otherwise "innocent" gate crasher.

My hosts were eager to introduce me to members of the high-hat crowd, but I begged off. I didn't fit with patricians. I nodded politely and even greeted a few people as I passed by on my way to the drinks and snacks table.

There, to my wondering eyes, did appear, a freshly opened bottle of *Sekt* – and *not* that cheap stuff one finds in grocery shops either! I opted for a sample before making a reconnaissance of the proffered snacks. After the first sip, I decided that I might desire another glass of *Sekt* prior to haunting the food array.

With fine wine, one does not rush. I'd enjoy every burst-of-flavor sip before getting a refill. To that end, I found an empty bistro table and parked.

"Ask me to dance."

I looked to my left and found myself at eye-level with two, hypnotic, doe eyes. She wore heels. Even without them she was taller than the norm. She had a funny face. Not funny *ha-ha*, but funny as in unexpectedly alluring. Her dark hair was cut boyishly short and parted neatly over her right ear. She was hardly a "knock out," but her posture and demeanor magnified her modest attributes exponentially.

"I make it a rule never to dance with anyone to whom I've not been properly introduced."

I was, I admit, very weary. I am not a person normally targeted by youngish and lithe ladies at top-drawer affairs. I noticed her wedding ring. It was, like its owner, attractive but not garish.

"You're not German," she concluded from my rusty tongue.

"Perceptive women make me nervous. Unnamed and perceptive women frighten me."

"Frau Osterhase," she announced, extending her right arm with comic rigidity.

It was a dare. Was she toying with me, or was she being insufferably rude?

"Herr Drinkwater," I responded.

Her thin lips exploded into a charming smile. She'd been caught out and knew it. Her arm never wavered. Dispensing with accepted protocol, I clasped her hand. Her grip was bold. This, more than her looks or carriage, made me like her – very much.

We left the bistro table and joined a half-dozen other couples doing the epileptic monkey – or whatever it was called. My social dancing had been consigned to the dustbin a decade or two prior. It was easy enough to shuffle my feet and make spastic movements with my hands and arms. Frau Easter Rabbit did the same, but her movements were graceful and practiced. She exuded confidence, but she never looked directly at me. Her eyes stared blankly over my left shoulder at nothing. The subdued, electric-echo music ceased after a short while.

"Thank-you, Herr Drinkwater," she smiled.

It was nearer a grimace than a smile. The chords in her lovely neck bulged. However, her expression lacked anguish. In truth, it radiated an unexpected charm.

Before I could respond, she turned gracefully to her right and walked purposefully toward a quartet of revelers. They had, apparently, witnessed the entire episode. They did not appear hostile or resentful, but they were, obviously, very, very curious.

"How'd you get to know her?" My friend asked later.

"Who?"

"Don't be coy. You can't wear it. You know damned well who I mean. Your dancing partner."

It was a single dance lasting less than two minutes. He was correct, however. I knew damned well who he meant.

"She introduced herself as Mrs. Easter Bunny."

"Weeeellll, she's no Easter rabbit, I assure you," he stated with tons of disbelief in his voice.

"That was Meike Kastner," his wife volunteered. "She's about the biggest name in the made-for-TV movie market – and not just here. She's dubbed herself into English and French for the heathens."

I was surprised, but not shocked. The woman had an aura about her, to be certain. She did not, however, possess the practiced snobbery of we mere mortals. I liked her for herself and not for her fame; a fame that had eluded me because I'd been so long removed from the German entertainment industry.

The greatest thing about being a consultant is that the customer of today knows bullshit. Of course, the company expects me to stick to the script. I do. When the company line has been exhausted, we change gears. The customer details concerns, and I plot out solutions. Most of them are successful. When they aren't, some local brain (there's always one) sketches out a scenario. From there, we all pitch in until all the problems are both addressed and resolved.

Of course, I'm the smartest man in the world. That's what I tell the head office. In reality, a dozen concerned purchasers are a damned sight better at helping *me* understand my company's product than those who, foolishly, hired me. Whenever I leave a trouble spot, I know more than I did when I arrived.

In Dubrovnik, I opted to rest my exhausted brain cells for a few hours. Prior to the evening meal at the hotel, I watched three ancient Popeye cartoons dubbed in Italian (as far as I could tell). Following a satisfying meal, I paused long enough for a B and S with a coffee chaser. Back in my warm and comfy room, I turned on the tube.

Popeye was, apparently, finished for the night. In his place I watched a trim, young woman walking away from me in a trendy dress. She wore shoes with very long, staccato heels. She, obviously, didn't feel comfortable in them; she treaded cautiously, resembling a loaded hay cart lurching over a rutted road.

There was a woman dubbing all female conversation into Croatian, and a man dubbing all the males (including children). This arrangement was comical enough to keep me from less entertaining pursuits. After three minutes or so, the camera provided a closeup of the woman in the staccato heels. It was the familiar and unmistakable funny face of Frau Osterhase!

I settled in for an assault in Croatian, but the words were all Greek to me. There was nothing wrong with the video, however. It was first-class, German filming and editing. It was an insipid girl-meets-guy, girl-hates-guy, guy-helps-girl, girl-falls-in-love-with-guy and etc. until, after several interludes in Italy (or Spain), guy-falls-in-love-with-girl and the happily-ever-after bit. I imagine that the dialogue in German (or English) would be insufferable. However, there is no escaping the certainty that Meike Kastner photographs well. She is not beautiful, but she is high-quality "cute." She projects the persona of a person no one wishes to hurt.

Here's an item for computer people to calculate: how many variations of *Pride and Prejudice* are possible? Novelists and screen writers have been laboring away for two-hundred years, and they have yet to exhaust the possibilities. Though I could never imagine Meike Kastner as Elizabeth Bennett, she needn't try. She had a screen image that is best described as "magnetic."

Some weeks later, in Riga, I was scouring the *Financial Times* when I found an incongruous filler. It is my habit to bypass such tripe, but my eye caught a familiar name: Kastner!

The actress confessed that she has reached the point in her career where she can choose her own projects. She preferred romance films and mini-series because "they are so rewarding."

Frau Osterhase!

Here was an unexpected insight. Frau Osterhase, a.k.a. Meike Kastner liked to chase dreams – even if they're scripted.

Why did I give a damn? I cannot hazard a guess, but I did.

I know it's happened to others. I've heard or read several examples, but I never experienced it until my Berlin initiation. Before that night, I never heard of Meike Kastner – had, in fact, no clue as to her existence. Suddenly and unbidden, she asks for (nay, demands) a dance during which she studiously ignored me. Next, I see her on Croatian TV. Then, I find a short blurb about her in the *Financial Times.*

Suddenly, I hear her name and see her image in a myriad of venues. I began collecting information about her like lint on a new suit – and just as unintentionally.

Meike was born in East Berlin eight years before the Wall crumbled. She participated in a rock band though she neither played a legitimate instrument nor sang anything other than backup for the featured vocalist. However, she wrote three or four numbers for inclusion in the band's repertoire.

Well, okay. I can see why a fledgling group would want Meike as window dressing. She was certain to attract attention. However, it was too much of a reach for me to accept her as a song writer. I mean – well, one must be able to read music and know all about counterpoint and all the Beethoven-like minutia before composing. However, for a rock band, I suppose being able to repeat the same chord thirty times is enough.

In Dresden, I found myself presenting the company spiel to a gathering of disinterested underlings. They were there because they were *told* to be there by the pooh-bahs. If it was a trial for them to sit through a mandatory meeting, imagine how I felt as the key presenter.

During a coffee break, I snapped up a juice and a glass provided by the conference center and retreated to an empty table. I expected to be avoided by the attendees. However, the table area was not plentiful enough to designate a "pest house." I was joined by two dour people. One was male; the other was not.

I tried to be convivial. They tried as well.

"Did you watch Meike Kastner last night in that – *Dingsta*?" The gloomy man asked of his co-worker.

"Oh, yes," the portly woman replied with a smug expression. "I know her."

"Really?" the man asked, obviously impressed.

"We studied opera together, once upon a time."

"Opera?"

The woman nodded.

"Neither of us lasted long," the woman reported, suddenly modest. "She didn't have the range, and I didn't have the stamina."

Here was a void. I hate quiet. It means I'm being snubbed – not without reason, but it's annoying, nonetheless.

"Last time I was in Berlin, I danced with her."

Bingo! With fewer than a dozen words, I went from pariah to featured celebrity.

Our afternoon session went swimmingly.

Never trust the press.

This dictum was established after years of experience. In my early days with the company, I did a lot of PR work. The suits insisted that I was personable and articulate. However, my words – carefully chosen and meticulously employed – were inevitably amended to meet the expectations or biases of the scribe or his employer. Data and breaking down concepts, problems and resolutions are too much for the simple minded. They want to meet a deadline and get to the bar early while the snacks are plentiful.

I scanned the *Financial Times* when abroad and the *WSJ* when at home. Even then, I took reports with a healthy dose of salt. Similarly, when I encountered anecdotes or biographical snippets *vis a vis* Meike Kastner, I treated them with deep suspicion. Of course, stories about her were both legion and entertaining, but they could be light-years removed from corroborated information. I had neither the time nor the inclination to run them down.

My verification of Meike's opera training – well, let's say curiosity and opportunity "just happened" to run together one afternoon. Not that I went out of my way to check up – well not very far out of my way. It was *hardly* out of my way.

Enough!

Meike began her "acting" career by appearing in short safety sketches on a kiddie show. She was in her late teens. She caught the eye of a casting director and was after "promoted" with a part in a long-running soap. They envisioned her as a pouty sneak and mischief-maker to frustrate the lives of her schoolmates.

It didn't "test" well.

Just when Meike thought she was about to get the push, the writers decided to change course. She was orphaned, adopted by a wealthy family, and was written into the Cinderella bit. She went along only because the pay was good. Moreover, it delayed enrolling in secretarial school.

Two years later, she tested for – and got – the lead in a "telenovel," a thirty-cent word for "high-class soap." She was the peasant girl who made good in business, fell in love, and married the boss's son. That took another two years. When she departed the show through a "happily-ever-after," she was replaced with – wait for it – a different, younger peasant girl.

I guess the boss can have as many sons as the writers can invent. The soap continues to run, in Germany, four other European countries, Brazil, and South Africa.

No, I do not reveal my sources.

I was nearing the end of my European dog-and-pony seminars. There remained three more "presentations" following a twelve-day hiatus. I opted to spend that time with my friends in Berlin. Full marks for planning, but a scrub out for coordination. My friends had fled to the Adriatic for fresh air and sun. Damn! I'd just left there.

I eschewed hotels since I couldn't justify them on my expense account. There were several apartments let by the week – little more than college dorm rooms, really. Regardless, I didn't require pampering. To underscore this sentiment, my first-night's evening meal was herring filets from a tin. The pull tab snapped off, and I accessed my "meal" by beating the container on the radiator until I was able to pry it open.

After a morning on Museum Island, I broke for lunch not far from the *Friedrichstrasse* station in the former Eastern Sector. It was hardly top-drawer, but it was clean and quiet. The service, and those providing it, were prompt and friendly. The *Jaeger Schnitzel* and beer would be my major meal of the day. I promised to scarf up a *Wurst* in the evening before returning to my digs.

"Herr Drinkwater?"

I looked up to discover a man of average height and looks. Beside him, like a colossus, was a hulking figure with a scar over his left eye. This menacing creature was certainly a man to make the boldest paladin stand aside.

Drinkwater? What the hell . . .?

Then, I realized.

Balls!

A jealous husband!

This was exactly what I didn't need. I, most certainly, did not need his muscle-bound enforcer.

"You danced with my wife," he reminded, needlessly.

I gulped. My power of speech had fled.

"I'm Lepple," he continued. "Walter Lepple. Meike's husband."

This was not the accepted protocol among Germans. First names were not bandied about among near strangers. This trifling sample of cultural habits crossed my panicked mind as I, involuntarily, eyed the gangland goon at his side.

"This is Herr Wagner," Lepple explained.

It's so nice to know the name of the person assigned to make mush of one's face. I didn't stand. If this bone-breaker was going to make me bleed, I might as well remain seated.

"May we . . .?"

I nodded and gestured. Perhaps, just maybe, I could negotiate my way out of this mess.

"I apologize, Herr Drinkwater. I saw you here alone and I felt obligated."

I glanced at the man and his silent sidekick.

Lepple chuckled softly.

"I apologize, again, Herr Drinkwater. This is not a confrontation. Herr Wagner is a movie stuntman. He and his wife are family friends of ours since – since, when Wagner?"

The silent man-mountain furled his brow.

"Six years, at least," he replied.

His voice was soft – very soft. It was as threatening as a puppy's yelp.

"My wife – it was a shoot-out, understand. Herr Wagner got five minutes of screen time in the film. A drunken, doped up goon with a gun. He shoots Meike's husband dead, then shoots her. She had a gun – don't ask me how, I never watch her *projects* . . ."

"She'd never fired a gun before," Wagner interrupted. "She'd never even held one. So, I worked with her until she looked like a woman who was used to handling guns. The three of us had a lot of laughs when I went to the house and trained her."

"Frau Wagner came over, too," Lepple continued. "She wanted to meet Meike. They got along right from the start. Meike has a knack for making friends."

I was beginning to relax. I remained on guard and ready to sprint at the first hostile action, but the situation did not seem as dire as I'd first feared.

"Such as, coercing a stranger to dance?"

I was taking a chance, of course, but my worst fears were fading.

Lepple smiled.

"We'd been arguing about some – thing. I can't remember. It was, probably my fault. Meike wanted to set me down a peg or two. She's not a vindictive person, Herr Drinkwater. Message received: we went to the party to have fun; not to fight."

I swallowed.

"My name is Matt Miller," I announced. "When – your wife introduced herself as Easter Rabbit, I responded with the first nonsense to enter my head."

Both men chuckled.

"Well played, Herr Miller," Lepple congratulated. "I'm certain she enjoyed that."

In a flash, I recalled that enigmatic smirk Meike Kastner sent my way during our mutually spurious introductions.

Lepple and Wagner joined me for lunch. We had a very nice conversation that covered several topics. Lepple was not in "the business." He managed three hardware supply outlets. He and Meike met when he brought a load of supplies to an exterior location on the Elbe. They took a fancy to each other and *zu veiter.* He was seldom recognized by the general public, but Wagner and a myriad of other players and production people called him Herr Kastner, an appellation he did not mind.

Herr Wagner was but one of many "co-stars" who found Meike both charming and convivial. He detailed the film for which he coached Meike in the use of firearms. It was her favorite story, though she didn't care for the way it was written.

Meike and her husband were part of a security contingent for an aircraft company. They were driving to work (or home) when they encountered a hopped-up drunk brandishing a pistol. They attempt to subdue the man (Wagner) who shoots them both and is, in turn, shot dead by Meike. Her husband dead, and Meike critically injured, she endures several operations and months of rehab. She is physically and emotionally traumatized. Finally, released from hospital, the widow simply goes through the motions returning to life. Of course, she meets a new man, and her will to live is revived.

"The shooting scene was the last thing they filmed," Wagner informed me. "It took nearly four hours to shoot a two-minute scene. Poor Meike was writhing around in mud and water half that morning. They'd get her dried off, into a clean costume, and put her back down on the street again – three times."

"She never told them," Lepple added. "She was pregnant with our first child. The producers prayed mightily after the fact. Had anything happened to the baby, Meike could have sued them for more money than the earth can supply."

Wagner shook his head.

"She'd never," he announced. "She could have said something at any time. She would have shouldered all the blame."

Lepple became sheepish.

"Had I known," he insisted. "I'd have put my foot down."

Wagner chuckled softly.

"He keeps close tabs on his wife's doings, now."

"My lawyers and I made it very clear: no violent scenes. They can use a stunt double, but no more crawling around on the ground or being roughed up by the likes of *Bully Boy* here."

Wagner chuckled again. He was frequently cast as a brute because he looked the part. In truth, however, he was gentle and caring. His wife was less than a hundred and sixty centimeters in height with a lithe and light build – and "not a bruise on her," according to Herr Lepple.

Eighteen months later, I camped in Germany on my way to Poland and Slovenia. I needed a few essentials. According to the concierge, I'd find an *Apotheke* several blocks away. He was both willing and able to secure my simple needs and deliver toothpaste, aspirin (100 mg), and an over-the-counter pain killer. Cramped from my flight, I opted for some welcome exercise. Alas, the welcome sensation of exercising my legs was soon overpowered by a sudden dose of fatigue. I turned into a "mega-store" and enjoyed the escalators for three flights. I found what I needed, paid, and was descending when I noticed a display of CDs.

Being experienced in crossing time zones, I realized I'd have some while before slumber would creep up on me. I paused to have a browse. My computer was set for region two, so any European DVD would do. I hadn't expected to see any of Meike's work, but there was a large collection, clearly marked. It was part of a "local-artists-who-made-good" promotion.

I was amazed at the number of East Berliners who'd cut a wide swath after Reunification.

Most of the wares were Meike's "novella" series, but there were a few of her made-for-TV productions. I wasn't in the mood for a *Pride-and-Prejudice* rip off, but I bought a copy of her "shoot-'em-up" if only to match it against what her husband and his stunt-man friend had told me.

The first ten minutes were enough.

Bang! Bang! Bang!

Meike writhing in the mud and goo next to her dead husband. Her struggle to charge her gun and place two well-aimed shots into the chest of Herr Wagner. He was very obliging; he stood stock still and let her blast him into the side of a dumpster where he slid to the ground and his death.

There followed her tedious recovery. The struggle with physical pain, the physical therapy regimen and the battle to learn how to walk again – the flowers, the cards at her bedside, the pablum she was forced to ingest, and the "quiet hours" when she wallowed in flashbacks of her life with her dead husband. Then, of course, the bitterness and emptiness of her life during hospital confinement and the toil of rehabilitation, followed by the emptiness of a home devoid of her husband. Then, according to the formula, flashbacks to happier days and the restless nights of despair until – ta da! – she meets a new guy and – *zu weiter.*

It was fun to watch Meike, but the story was tedious and formulaic. During the entire film, I asked myself *why a shootout*? It was hardly mentioned. An *Autobahn* accident would have served as well, if not better. I concluded somebody owed Herr Wagner a favor, so he got a few seconds on screen, a hand-full of Euros, and his name in the credits. However, he and his wife become fast friends with Meike and her husband, an unscripted and felicitous consequence.

I shall always have a soft spot in my heart for Frau *Osterhase*, but – if the one film I watched is representative – her movie career remains undistinguished if lucrative. Her name draws TV viewers by the millions. She's a recognized celebrity in Germany, the neighboring European countries, and Latin America.

I understand some producer wanted her to belt out a tune during one of her formula romances. Meike refused. According to her husband, she considers herself a failure as a singer. Of course, she strikes me as intelligent enough to realize that tried-and-true maxim: if it ain't broke, don't fix it.

Rediscovering Old Friends

I don't recall when I got the chess bug. My parents got me a set of pieces and a checkerboard one Christmas. I learned the moves, but my age was still in the single digits. The only person I could play with was my dad (not what he intended, I'm sure). I would get very angry whenever I lost - which was, roughly, every game. Because I made such a production over my defeats, Dad refused to play.

The chess pieces were integrated into my toy-soldier army and were subject to battle after battle. I never lost. Of course, I was the only general engaged, so these victories were simply a matter of filling time while waiting for the next comic book or the next scale model aircraft.

Over the years, I would come across a chess set and couldn't resist setting them up and having a go. Playing both sides in a game precluded my ever losing. Because white always had the first move, I favored that side. I would get petulant whenever I discovered that I was playing the black pieces better. I never threw a fit, but I recall throwing a chess piece or two when black won.

Padded cells were created with me in mind.

Once in a great while, I found someone who was eager to play. I'd show him (it was always a "him") how to move the figures preparatory to beating the neophyte. Though I had only played against Dad and myself, I realized that experience provided a decided edge.

By the time I entered high school, I was a chess duffer. I didn't seek a game, but I'd sit down if the opportunity arose. I was never any good - only good enough to hold my own. The games were never serious. We'd spend most of our time telling stories, reciting childish jokes, or listening to music.

I bought a book about chess openings. I learned something I should have figured out for myself: he (or she) who controls the four, center squares had the better game and the best chance of winning. The book also advised against moving the same piece twice in the opening stages of the game. I never really understood this one. The sample lines of play in the book provided a myriad of violations of this rule. Further, these examples were made by masters and grand masters. Many of their moves were baffling! I couldn't understand how these giants of the game could eschew (what appeared to me) brilliant moves in order to play something innocuous.

I would put the book aside and play both sides of a game's remainder, proving that my moves were far superior to those of the "experts." With the passage of time, and after further study, I realized the really good players had either played or studied games where my "superior and brilliant moves" were used. Without exception, they were discarded because, ultimately, they led to disaster.

When I went to college, I played with my fraternity brothers from time to time. I won far more often than I lost because I was so "wise." I'd play for the center squares and develop my pieces while my poor-schmuck opponents liked to move the rook pawns and get their rooks into the game first.

Suckers!

Whenever someone opened with pawn to rook four, I knew the game was as good as won. After the eighth move, I'd have my side ready to attack while my hapless friend had only three or four soldiers off their original squares.

I thought I was hot (chess) stuff –

Until the Fischer, Spassky match of '72.

My fellow ancients may well remember a time when one couldn't watch any news or sports report without getting the latest on the biggest thing in chess since – well, forever!

The college library had back issues of chess periodicals. I studied several and discovered there were such things as speed-chess tournaments in addition to the major, prestigious events around the world. I specifically remember seeing a cartoon featuring Spassky looking very smug and confident conferring with a harried looking "trainer."

"But, Boris," the caption read. "What if he *doesn't* play P-K4?"

Ruy Lopez: I remembered it from my chess opening books. I was curious about it, but I didn't know enough to play it. After 3. B-QKt5, black could play P-QR3. That necessitates the violation of the don't-move-the-same-piece-during-the-opening rule. However, it was a move-it- or-lose-it proposition. If I moved 4. B-R4 and black played P-QKt. 4, I'd be forced to move the bishop to knight three where it would be of little use.

If I were either Fischer or Spassky, I would understand why an experienced player would not play pawn to knight four. I, however, wasn't (and still "amn't") a grandmaster or, even, a master; I didn't (and don't) know why. Therefore, I was reluctant to play the Ruy Lopez as white. However, when playing black, I *always* played 4. . . . P-QKt. 4: my "chase the bishop" ploy.

I continued to play and win more than I lost. It was fun to win, but frustrating to lose.

"How could I be so stupid?" I'd admonish myself.

I learned, eventually, to watch the knights. Before I contemplated any move, I would study my opponent's knights. Those bastards are tricky. Whenever I developed (what fighter pilots call) "target fixation," I'd get excited and carry out an attack – forgetting, momentarily, the enemy knights. Frequently, I'd find myself in a fork. If my opponent placed a knight where it attacked two of my men, one of them must die. If the knight put my king in check and I couldn't capture it, I was forced to move the king. If a knight simultaneously attacked my king *and* queen – game over. This happened more than once.

After college, I couldn't find work in my chosen field. Too lazy to get honest work, and too determined to travel in Europe, I joined the Army. In addition to a "guarantee" of a European posting, I was offered a twenty-five-hundred-dollar bonus if I selected a combat-arms MOS. Because I had attended college, I went into service as an E-3; that is Army speak for Private First Class. Not only was I senior to every other "'cruit" in my training company, I got the "big bucks" on payday. That is a hollow boast. An E-3's pay is plenty anemic, believe me. However, when compared with the E-1s and E-2s, it was a princely sum.

Basic training at Fort Leonard Wood and advanced training at Fort Polk. I didn't wear my rank during training because I didn't want to set myself up as a target, either from the drill sergeants or my fellow trainees. Following training, I was sent to Fort Bliss for Redeye training, learning to use a shoulder-fired anti-aircraft weapon. Upon graduation, I was allowed thirty days. I spent part of it with my family. The remainder I spent driving around the Civil War battlefields of Fredericksburg, Chancellorsville, and the Wilderness. Next to chess, the Civil War was my hobby.

All that E-3 pay I earned, plus the two thousand Uncle Sugar awarded me (the five-hundred-dollar difference, my uncle grabbed for "taxes") really burnt a hole in my pocket. Airfare, car rental, and hotel rooms were handled with ease.

As an aside, I was in a Richmond hotel when a commercial came on for a clothing store (I think). The cute little come-hither girl I recognized instantly. She and I graduated from the same university. I knew she wanted to be a model. I'd see her in mail-order catalogues from time to time, but this was the only time I ever saw her on the tube. AFN Europe doesn't run commercials.

In the air defense section of the combat support company, there was one officer, one staff sergeant, one buck sergeant, one specialist (E-4), eight PFCs, privates (E-2) and privates (E-1). That single specialist was Dusty, a mustachioed gent with the military bearing of a civilian. I only heard him give one command. It was after retreat and just prior to mail call. The officer and two sergeants were absent for reasons unknown. That left Dusty, as the ranking man, to stand in front of our motley crew. When the first sergeant dismissed the troops, Dusty did a snappy about face and addressed us.

"Section! Scatter to the four winds, Ho!"

We didn't need to be told twice.

As I ambled over to the mess hall, I realized Dusty was a man after my own heart.

My one military objective was to keep my weekends free. Inevitably, I'd have to pull CQ periodically, but could ill afford "extra duty." Being "more Army" than others in my section required very little effort. Within ten weeks, I was promoted to specialist (E-4), the same day I was assigned to KP. Only E-3s and below were tapped for KP, but I didn't complain. I'd just got a boost in pay, and my weekend remained free.

It took me over a year to discover that there was somewhere other than Heidelberg to spend a weekend. I'd head out on a Friday afternoon and return on Sunday afternoon. I'd spend two nights in a bed-and-breakfast or a tourist hotel and either explore the town or revisit favorite spots. The babble in a dozen languages and the young women (particularly in the summer months) were exceedingly intoxicating.

Back "home," in the barracks, I started with a room of my own. As our section strength grew, I hosted a few roommates. Most of the "new guys" were interested in booze and pot. We slept in the same room, stood inspection, kept our room up to the first-sergeant's standards, and took our turn cleaning up and hosing down the latrine area.

I was a buck sergeant by the time Dusty was assigned to my room. He was still a specialist-fourth, but he was something of a pain in the ass on the company level. We, however, got along fine. He did his drinking downtown or in the EM Club. If he doped, I never caught him. His specialty (pardon the pun) was speaking bluntly and, often, without waiting to be recognized.

I'd just bought an electric coffee pot from someone rotating back to the States. I was, also, a new owner of *The Fireside Book of Chess*, a volume (I think) I bought at the base bookstore. Dusty offered to buy half the coffee if he could drink half the pot. When he caught me reading my book (there were articles and short stories in addition to a myriad of notable games), he expressed an interest. Within the week, we had a chess board and pieces. Two or three weeks later, I discovered (in Heidelberg) a travel case: a hinged chess board containing wooden pieces. We could take this treasure out in the field with us on maneuvers (though we never did).

Dusty gave the book a cursory look and attempted to solve some of the contrived problems contained therein. I, however, played through several of the games – the best the grandmasters had to offer. Steinitz, Lasker, Capablanca, Alekhine, and the enigmatic Morphy were heavily represented. Many, if not most, of the games began with 1. P-Q4.

I was never comfortable with that. I always started with the king's pawn. It's what I knew.

I'd have the board out and be playing through a game. When Dusty came in, he'd grab the coffee pot and fetch fresh, cold water. With the el cheapo coffee pot gurgling (remember percolators?), I'd tune to AFN, and we'd listen to the radio as we played.

There were, on weekdays, old, half-hour radio shows. My favorite was *The Life of Riley* with Bill Bendix and John Brown, the next-door neighbor who was, also, the voice of Digby O'Dell, "The Friendly Undertaker." This was the Thursday offering; I forget the others. These entertainments distracted me far more than they did Dusty.

I was the better player, but my mind wandered. When I lost, it was because of one of those damned knights. It became a fetish. If I had half a chance, I'd sacrifice a bishop for a knight without qualm. I think I sacrificed my queen once, just to clear the board of Dusty's knights.

Eventually, Dusty became a short timer. His interest in becoming a civilian interrupted our, otherwise, placid existence. If he made a bonehead move, I'd scold him. If he couldn't play a good game, there was no point in setting up the board.

"Hey!" he'd respond. "I'm so short, I have to stand on a nickel to see over a dime."

Due to his attitude, we reversed seniority. I was a buck sergeant while he left for the States as a mosquito wing (Private E-2). He didn't give a rat's ass, but I was left without a sparring partner. Occasionally, other barracks mates would sit down to play with me, but they were all neophytes. I got no pleasure in dispatching these "beginners" in fifteen moves (or less). I was reduced to re-playing the games in *The Fireside Book of Chess.*

Over time, watching (vicariously) these masters at work grew stale.

Decades later, my son asked me what I'd like for Christmas. Without a moment of hesitation, I requested a copy of *The Fireside Book of Chess.* Of course, these days, it was only an internet search away.

After years and years and years, I have my old friend back. It's at my elbow as I type (dare I use that archaic word?). I've re-read the stories, resolved the problems, and replayed nearly every game. When I finish, I'll return to the copyright date and begin anew. I haven't found a chess partner (yet), but coffee and old-time radio shows remain an integral part of my chess pleasure.

Smuggler

It would require a thousand, shrill tongues a thousand hours to narrate or recount or describe the stark, empty hours of deep-space travel. Until we reached Titan, there was little to do to pass one idle hour after another and another and another! Oh, the geniuses who conjured the technology, science, and invented the materials to make the journey possible were (are) peerless engineers. They fooled themselves (and us) into thinking that they were, also, masters of psychology and human behavior.

Well, to their credit, they had foresight enough to include two "supernumeraries" on our mission. These "observers" (mission-control parlance for "dead weight") were compiling mountains of data to transmit back to Mother Earth in addition to the notes and observations of the crew (including themselves) for future evaluation by the shrinks and sociologists.

We were one year into the mission, nearly three quarters of the way to our objective and just under a third of the mission as planned. There were twelve of us. We were the guinea pigs. Future missions would be built around our experience. To qualify for the Titan Mission, a person had to be young, in excellent health, an endurance athlete, and have just the "right" psych profile. Ten of us had to be scientists. However, these "experts," including myself, were decidedly *not* major names in our field of expertise.

I'm a geologist. My degree says so. However, I'm not bold enough to describe myself as an expert. I can (and did) tick off the names of seven classmates who were superior geologists. Well, they didn't measure up to the physical demands. Therefore, on all future resumes, I could boast of being the "Team Leader of the Titan Expedition."

For certain, I was eager to go. What geologist would pass up a chance to explore a virgin landscape. I shall be a footnote in ten thousand monographs for decades. Unfortunately, my findings, hypotheses, and conclusions would be erased the moment a *real* scientist gets a crack at the Titan terrain.

We were required to submit to eighteen hours of isolation. We were allowed a toilet, a supply of packaged food, unlimited water, a reclining chair, and a blanket. However, we were, otherwise, cut off from the rest of creation.

The more cynical among us called it the "think tank." However, the purpose was exceptionally mundane. We were cut off from all possible distractions so we could focus all our attention on a single question: Do you *really* want to spend four years of your life in space?

I smuggled in two paperback books to help me pass the time. My mind was made up before I went into purgatory. Eighteen hours would not make a difference – not to me. However, nearly two thirds of the candidates emerged from isolation to announce, "Hell, no!"

There was a myriad of activity at the earth-orbit station and for the first several hours after our departure. After that, we were largely reduced to twisting knobs, monitoring systems and making minor repairs as required. The computers were running the ship; all we had to do was hang on. Of course, we must keep busy or go bonkers. We took turns standing "watches." We had to make certain our reactor functioned properly, that our air was being properly scrubbed and recycled and renewed (boosted artificially) to remain within exacting tolerances. Our trash (and body waste) had to be stored until ejected – an exciting procedure which must be done "just so," or the ejecta would play havoc with our commo systems. We had two "suitcases" flying in formation with us. They contained our consumables. One of them, when empty, would be sent crashing into Titan so the "brains" and our equipment could get seismic readings.

Twelve people confined to a small space constitutes the potential for eighteen political parties and a score of wars. It was inevitable that nerves would be strained and the social dynamic damaged. It was the job of the supernumeraries to soothe ruffled feathers before tempers flared. Unfortunately, the supernumeraries were people, too. They were as susceptible to becoming "space happy" as the rest of us. We were very aware of our fragility and followed the psyche "guidelines" religiously.

One of the "iron-clad" mission rules was that each crew member be allotted ninety minutes of "private time" per twenty-four-hour period. That's mission-rules speak for "back into isolation." During our "private time" we could not be disturbed for any reason short of a catastrophic "event" (mission-rules speak for "you gonna die").

Some people used their "private time" for a nap. Others caught up on sending and receiving messages. Some played video games. We all took turns reading the books we brought (we each were allowed six books of our choice, copied onto thin paper and bound in lightweight, plastic covers). In addition, we could request additional materials sent up by the comm link, but we'd require our personal devices to read them. I, as with most of my crewmates, liked to "turn pages." These almost-real books were, therefore, seldom left unattended. Who could predict how many times we would read the same book? Speaking only for myself, I re-read only my favorite pages; I suspected others of doing the same.

Whenever I'm banished to my "quarters," (a space-travel euphemism for my assigned hovel – the exact copy of the "quarters" assigned to my fellow crewmen and crewwomen), I shed my footwear, remove my "flight suit" and send it down the laundry chute. I pull out my "clean" flight suit to let it air out a little. I've grown used to the faint chemical scent – hardly notice it anymore.

I rub myself down with the sanitation "goo," recalling how the ancient Romans liked to use olive oil and a "scraper" for the same purpose. I've nothing to scrape away the grime. The quick dispersing chemical is carried away, along with any toxins, for filtering, reclamation, scrubbing and recycling.

I wrap myself in a lightweight robe, recline on my "bunk," brace my feet against my door (a.k.a. "hatch"), and call up an arbitrary radio episode. I can select from scores at will, but I never do. Let it be a surprise.

I spend most of my mandatory isolation listening to old radio broadcasts.

My grandfather collected recordings of old-time radio shows. Some were on discs. That will give you a clue as to the technology leaps since his time.

Before we left, I downloaded a plethora of old shows – programs my crew never dreamed existed.

I had twenty episodes each of

Gunsmoke
Have Gun Will Travel
Fort Laramie
Our Miss Brooks
Father Knows Best

Fibber McGee and Molly
Jack Benny
Ozzie and Harriet
The Aldrich Family
Richard Diamond
Dragnet
Information Please
Lum and Abner

There were others.

I'll not waste my "private time" in taking inventory.

Further, I can (and have) requested another twenty episodes of my favorites sent up periodically. It drives mission control mad. They must find some antique person to search for antique recordings. Then, they must translate them into computer lingo before sending them. Normally, several days elapse before my requests are filled. So what? I'm not going anywhere (only to Titan).

I never tire of listening to these ancient programs. I can sit up, lay down, or exercise while listening. It matters not that I know the stories, jokes, musical selections, or dialogue by heart; I revel in the voices. During my sleep period, I often doze while re-listening to a program.

I'm the butt of many crew jokes. I was eccentric enough as the mission rock-pounder. Obviously, my penchant for a medium long dead qualifies me to be the mission whack-a-doodle. They constantly prod me and suggest more modern and "engaging" entertainments. I, frequently, pretend to relent. Yes, I'll announce, I'll watch an episode of *Smoot* or play a round of *Treasure Hunt*. Even with the best intentions of keeping my word, I'm distracted for only a few minutes. The images of my imagination are far more vivid and immediate than anything video stories or games provide. Also, when listening, I maintain my equipment or tend to personal hygiene without missing a word. Video requires monitoring. I do enough of that during my assigned watches.

Dr. Simpson is a biochemist and the mission barber. It's very tricky to cut hair in space and in a .7 g environment. We cannot afford to have hair floating around and, possibly, finding its way into some of our more sensitive equipment. We must make an appointment, and the "client" must help assemble the proper "shelter." It doesn't take long, but, as on earth, the barber tends to chat up the customer.

"What's with you and those awful radio shows?" she asks me.

"Practice."

"Come again?"

"We're on a mission to explore and catalogue an alien world."

"If we ever get there," she replied.

"I don't know what life was like in the 30s, 40s, and 50s," I remind her. "Listening to these old shows, I've learned tons of things about ancient life."

"Yeah? So?"

"I especially like the Gunsmoke episodes when Matt and Chester ride across the empty prairie. I can imagine what it must be like, all that vastness with no bulkheads, no LS suits, no boundaries. Even with a vehicle, it would take hours to get to the horizon – and they only had horses."

She made a noise. Dr. Simpson frequently spoke with grunts and moans. This one communicated thoughtfulness.

"I like the shows where people are in houses. I picture them in my mind. There's always a stairway. There are several rooms, and I picture each one. Best of all, the people can leave the house and go off to other places. All they need to do is open a door and walk out. Sometimes, that's all they do; they just go out for a walk. I picture trees and flowers and grass and birds – the Gunsmoke program has lots of animal sounds: dogs, horses, coyotes, birds – they even go fishing sometimes and there's water sounds and splashes."

No sound this time. Dr. Simpson was probably suffering from withdrawal. We all suffer from time to time, but I, apparently, don't endure as often or as deeply as the others.

"Write it up," she dared me. "I'll pass it around and we'll evaluate your work."

She'd like that. The crew, probably, would as well. We are itching to get on with the mission, but it's a long, long bus ride to work. We all seek diversions.

"It's therapeutic as well," I appended. "Whenever I get the urge to go out for a walk, I just take a spin around the neighborhood with my radio friends. You'd be surprised how vivid a picture you can form through audio clues and an active imagination."

She grunted, but I knew she was thinking.

"It seems to me that a person of this century would have to be properly trained in order to realize any benefit."

"Maybe, I could train you."

"Maybe," she concluded.

She was serious. I could tell by the way she enunciated that word. When you're trapped in a sardine tin for years, you'd be surprised how well you can know and understand your crewmates.

"It might take time and a lot of practice," I warned.

"My social calendar isn't very crowded," she reminded.

A proverbial tingle went up my spine. Dr. Simpson was *not* the woman I'd most want to be trapped on a desert island with. She did not have a face to stop a clock, but she'd slow it considerably. Further, she was rough in her manners, mode of expression, and her "laying on of hands," even with something as basic as cutting hair. However, she was a crewmate. If there was anything I could do to introduce her to a new, virtual world it might contribute to the success of our mission.

We'd perform our scientific tasks like the dedicated professionals we are. However, the major worry of mission planners is how a dozen people can be confined to a limited area for years without murdering each other. We all had our individual coping mechanisms and skills, but building new competencies is only prudent.

"Talk to me," I mutter to myself. "Don't show me; just talk."

I swear, I could endure a mission to another solar system so long as mission control can keep me supplied with audio. I can be alone without being alone.

Let the shrinks unravel that!

Remember When Redux

Denis Wagner pressed hard against the stone wall. Once it had served as an animal enclosure. A small, surviving portion remained relatively intact. The weapons of war had scattered the remainder hither and yon. It was dark, but the artillery burst illuminated the countryside quite sufficiently.

Wagner pressed hard against the section of wall which kept him safe from observation – or so he hoped. If the Germans were "over there," he was safe. If the wall was oblique to their lines, he was exposed. He figured, if he kept still, he'd escape detection. If he weren't, German forward observers might mistake him for a body. This latter possibility didn't provide any comfort. He'd heard of several GIs who would shoot dead Germans, "just to make certain."

Denis Wagner would give everything he had (precious little) to know where the company went to. He was assigned (loosely) to an infantry battalion but had advanced with a single company. As they neared Germany, the company was reduced to thirty or so soldiers and a slew of replacements who were wounded or killed with alarming frequency.

The German Army made it clear that the Yanks were not welcome. Wagner had experienced mortar fire before, but this barrage was laid down by guns – damned big guns.

Everyone dove for cover. Denis had two objectives: stay low and find cover. As a war correspondent, he was very much on his own. The company (what remained of it) was under the command of a salty NCO of the old school. He issued orders above the roar of the cannon and led the men – somewhere. Denis was alone and frightened. When the explosive shells ceased, he'd try to find the company. Alternatively, he might get the hell out and find the battalion CP. He reckoned that it was – "back there" – somewhere.

Denis did not want to be where he was, but he didn't want to move around. Even from his current location, he heard the disturbing *zing* and *whoosh* of shrapnel. These deadly missiles could be dozens of feet above his head, or they could be only inches away. If one of them struck him, it would hurt like blazes! It would be hot. In addition to slicing through his flesh, it would burn like hell. Of course, if a scrap of flying metal caught him just right, Denis would be deceased.

If that happened, he prayed it would be over in an instant.

He'd seen too many men for whom nothing could be done, who cried and screamed in pain for seemingly hours before Death gathered them up.

The BBC and the Army intelligence brains insisted that the Germans were on their heels. So long as the battalion kept its advance, armed resistance would be minimal.

Denis didn't understand how an artillery barrage of an hour or longer could possibly qualify as "minimal." Obviously, the Krauts had a shit-pile of ammo. Moreover, they had a very excellent idea of where the battalion was.

The moment the firing lifted, Denis could expect a counterattack. He really didn't want to be where he was when that happened. He'd love to race for the rear echelons and rest up a bit before hunting for "his company," but he had no firm idea which direction was the "rear." He had no map, no compass, no weapons, no food and very little water. He'd relied on the company and platoon leadership for those things.

A shell burst not thirty feet away. He heard *zings* and *whooshes* moments before a shower of dirt and crushed rock rained down upon him. In the flash of the burst, he noticed a silhouette of a man. He was crouched and moving fast. He sought cover. The meagre remains of the animal pen would have to serve.

"Keep down!" he yelled.

It was childish and silly. Who could hear over that racket? The unceasing bursts stuffed his ears sufficiently enough that he doubted he had any hearing left.

Suddenly, the flashes and the cacophony ceased. The ground no longer quaked and throbbed. He prepared to run – but in what direction? What of the figure he'd seen? It was down. Did that last burst sever an artery?

Cautiously, he peered over his impromptu parapet. He saw nothing. He heard nothing – not that he could hear a bass drum six feet away. Frantically, he scanned for any movement.

"Got a cigarette?"

He jumped and spun around.

The voice was female. She had shouted into the nearest ear.

Beside him, her face contorted and writhed in pain. The – person – pressed up against him. She wore a uniform devoid of insignia and a British helmet strapped on tight.

"Cigarette, damn you! You ain't Jerry. I can tell by lookin'. You're a Yank. Unless you're a bleeding imbecile, you speak English. Cigarette, blast yer eyes!"

Denis was working up to a proper panic. The shelling had lifted. Even a military neophyte realized troops would quickly fill the area. He didn't want to be captured. He didn't want to be killed by some trigger-happy German recruit. Nevertheless, he dug into his shirt pocket and produced a crumpled pack of Camels.

The woman's hands were shaking, but she captured a slightly bent cancer stick. She had her own matches.

"Not a good idea to light up," Denis advised. "The matches and the glow of that cig can be seen for miles. Some people around here are not very friendly."

"Save it, parson," she advised.

In the splash of light, he noticed the holstered pistol on her hip.

"Who the hell are you?" he demanded.

Was this woman deliberately attempting to get them killed?

"I'm paid by the Birmingham *Union*," she announced.

"Can't you send dispatches from further back? Correspondents aren't allowed to carry weapons."

"I took it off a dead tanker," she sputtered. "He won't be needing it."

Damn!

He looked around nervously. If the Krauts were on their way, they'd fire at anything that looked like a threat.

"What the hell do you think you're doing with it?"

"Giving myself options," she said, tearing franticly at a pant leg. "I can defend my virtue, or I can cash in. Won't know which – until – they force – my hand."

She struggled mightily until Denis heard the tearing of loose-fitting trousers two-sizes (at least) too large for her. She shifted until she was on her side, using Denis as both a cover from small arms fire and as something to lean against while doing – whatever she was doing.

The Birmingham reporter launched into a series of grunts and gasps punctuated by the most severe Anglo-Saxon oaths he'd ever heard. Finally, her hand jerked, and her body went limp. For a moment, he thought she'd passed out. Another string of whispered oaths escaped her, but her muted voice trembled. After several seconds, her hand tossed something aside. Denis heard a metallic clang when it hit a rock.

"I must be bleeding," she moaned. "Do you have something I can use for a compress?"

Indeed, he did. He had one in his "emergency pack." He hadn't intended to share it. He had a queer feeling that he might need it before the dawn came. After a thoughtful hesitation, Denis realized that his conscience would never give him peace if he allowed the woman bleed to death.

"You need a medic," he admonished.

"Taxi!"

She was in so much pain that her facetious remark was partially arrested by her clinched teeth.

Denis had no bedside manner. He was frightened. At any moment, a posse of very angry German soldiers would visit them. He didn't want to be there. Unfortunately, he couldn't run for his life and leave this brainless Brit to bleed out.

He struggled and fumbled. He used his belt as a tourniquet to help stem the flow. Now, he was stuck. He had to remain and relieve the pressure every so often or –

"That damned Russell!" she said, overpowering her noises of pain.

"Pardon?"

"That bastard who went to the Crimea for the *Times*! Then, he went to America to watch you people slaughter each other and write it all up for the tea and crumpets crowd. If it weren't for that puffed up popinjay, neither of us would be here now."

He was getting angry.

"I'm not so sure of that."

She lay back and arched her neck. The pain, and the bleeding, seemed to subside. Gradually, and with obvious effort, she put his cigarette between her lips.

"Got a light, Yank?"

Against his better judgement, he relit her Camel. After several desperate puffs, she struggled to sit up.

"Take that thing off and let's look."

The shrapnel had struck her mid-thigh. She could have lost the entire leg or severed the major artery. Apparently, that chunk of steel had lost most of its velocity by the time it found her. It hurt and burned like blazes, but the wound was little more than a scratch when compared to the damage it could have done.

She helped him dab away the blood. The hot, metal fragment "fried" the wound. The blood that did escape was beginning to clot. Slowly, with a trembling hand, she pressed the end of the cigarette into the wound.

"What the hell are you doing?" he snapped.

"Cauterizing. I'm damned if I'll get infection or blood poisoning."

"You need a medic," he repeated.

"Fetch me one. I'm not going anywhere."

It was painful to watch her. There was an encore of Anglo-Saxon invectives. She tried so hard to be stoic, but she let fly several expressions of pain I'm certain could be heard in Berlin.

The company – the "lost" company – couldn't have been more than a hundred yards away. The Germans, for some obscure reason, made no attempt to flank the GIs, else two correspondents would have fallen into their grip.

The firing reached a crescendo and began slackening – slightly.

"Have a cigarette?"

He turned away from the firefight to find the woman offering him her pack.

"Why did you ask *me* for a fag?" he demanded, resentfully.

"These are Egyptian," she informed, her hand still trembling. "They cost a fortune – when you're lucky enough to get them. You don't use these to treat wounds."

He fought down the urge to hit his fist with her face. He took one and lit up. A moment later, he lit hers. During a battle royale, they lay back and enjoyed a smoke.

Denis never experienced a better cigarette.

Denis Wagner was in the UK pimping his book about war-time London. He had only limited experience there during the war, but his research was exhaustive. He interviewed as many survivors of the Blitz as he could find; he spent weeks buried in government, military and civil archives. He haunted museums, pubs, neighborhoods, and any Home Guard personnel still alive and kicking.

He began his research in the late fifties. His book was published, in America, in 1966. A London publisher, with minor edits and revisions, reissued his manuscript two years later. The volume had sluggish sales in America, but the British – particularly Londoners – bought copious volumes. It seemed the purchasers either knew, or knew of, many people Wagner included in his book.

With a single exception, the reviews of Wagner's history were highly favorable. One of the more persnickety (and snooty) quarterlies praised Denis Wagner for his "sophisticated style and his pin-point vocabulary."

Douglas Newman was one of many who kept a finger on the pulse of the public. He was curious enough to buy a volume, though he could only read a page or two at a time. His schedule demanded most of his waking hours.

Remember When was caught flat. Sir Ian's presence was required in the House. They were prepared for such eventualities. The producer contacted Sara Newland-Attwood, Lady Harcourt. The twice divorced aristocrat was noted for her pen. She was a literary critic featured in two national publications, a columnist for the *Evening Watch,* and the authoress of two learned tomes on East Anglican history and heritage. Her life was littered with adventures, some tragic, many humorous. When she and Tommy Dunn crossed verbal swords, riotous laughter was certain to dominate.

In the preverbal "last minute," Colin Whitehouse was stricken and taken to hospital with a painful malady. The doctors agreed that he was sufficiently "cured" by a "health cocktail," but they insisted he remain a guest of National Health for several days.

Denis Wagner was in a studio in Bush House. Grasping at straws, Douglas Newman, being nearest, rushed up to the studio and intercepted Wagner the moment he emerged. There followed a spirited plea or, in Newman's words, begging mercy on bended knee.

Wagner was reticent, but he hated to see an otherwise dignified personage reduced to such dire circumstances.

The program would be recorded before a live audience in Portland Place. Armed with an official letter and identification number, Denis Wagner waited in the main lobby for only a few moments before a uniformed security person escorted him into a lift. Beads of sweat were forming on his forehead as his mute escort led him down a narrow hallway. Denis Wagner, at no time in his life, was described as a *raconteur*. Douglas Newman, however, twisted his arm on the mistaken conceit that he was, as an author and lecturer, the perfect person to round out the panel.

Denis had never heard the show. He'd harvested tiny slivers from nearby radios while engaged in other matters. It meant nothing to him. Since he could not be amusing and witty in the British fashion, he could either languish in embarrassed silence or die of embarrassment while attempting his American brand of humor.

Finally, he was ushered into a small yet tastefully decorated salon. He heard French. A man was speaking. Immediately upon entering, his “escort” abandoned him after closing the door behind him and, with it, sealing Denis off from the outside world.

A man in a white, single-breasted suit hefted himself out of a lounge chair of the Victorian style. His highly polished brown shoes were incongruous under all that white. His gaudy green and yellow striped tie shrieked buffoonery. The “ice cream man,” was Tommy Dunn. Even a provincial rube would recognize this world-famous comic. He was shorter and wider in real life, but he was scrubbed and polished without a strand of hair out of place.

“You are Denis Wagner,” he announced. “Just a tic.”

He turned to the table on the opposite side of the chair and snatched up a bound volume Denis recognized immediately.

“I’m a big fan of yours,” the comic announced. “I read your book in one go. I couldn’t put it down. I realize we haven’t been properly introduced, but would you do me the inestimable pleasure, and honor, of signing my copy?”

“You do know Tommy Dunn,” a female stated from her perch on a small couch opposite.

“One must travel very far not to know Tommy Dunn,” Wagner replied, hoping he’d be mistaken for someone with cosmopolitan credentials.

As he fumbled for the pen in his jacket pocket, he studied the woman. She was no spring chicken by any standard of measure, but she carried her years well. She sat in the composed posture of a British aristocrat. One white glove was firmly gripped, lengthwise, in the glove of her left hand. Her bare right hand was adorned with a pale orange polish, but the nails were cut very short.

Tommy Dunn, the consummate performer, was flustered and embarrassed.

“I’m so excited, I’ve forgotten my manners,” he said. “Denis Wagner, may I present Sara Newland-Attwood, Lady Harcourt.”

Wagner was in a quandary. The pen was in his hand. Should he offer it to the man so eager to have it, or should he give full attention to the aristocrat? She cued him by extending her naked hand.

"Sara Newland-Attwood," she said with practiced calm. "That's how my friends address me. Only my enemies call me *Lady* Harcourt."

"I trust that you are never addressed thus," he replied, taking her hand for only the briefest moment.

It was overdone. Denis made a note to bang his head against the wall of his hotel room later.

"I *am* addressed thus," she iterated. "Quite often, in fact."

"Pleased to meet you, Sara Newland-Attwood."

She smiled. It was genuine.

"I have not read your book," she continued. "It comes highly recommended. I fear that Tommy here will not allow me a moment's peace until I do read it. From what he's been telling me, I'm certain to find it well worth my while."

"I hope your expectations will not be unfounded."

She smiled again.

"I'm certain they will not be *unfounded*."

Now, the matter of the book signing.

"I heard French when I came in," Denis noted.

"Tommy is fluent," Sara Newland-Attwood informed. "I'm quite literate enough for daily use, but Tommy speaks like a native – so he tells me. I prefer speaking in French with Tommy. He doesn't do comedy in French. He's quite personable when speaking French. He's highly educated and very stimulating."

Tommy Dunn, the internationally well-known funny man, blushed visibly.

"I speak French, fluently," Denis reported while attempting to compose a worthy sentiment for inclusion in his book. "However, my fluency is restricted to a half dozen words – none of which can be used with any of the others."

Tommy chuckled. Denis suspected he was filing this report away for possible future use.

Clive Martin arrived.

Here we go, Denis thought.

Apparently, however, comedians do not have to be funny when not working. Denis expected a "can-you-top-this?" joust. Instead, Tommy and Clive conversed with all the decorum of a pair of Oxford Dons.

"I bought your book, yesterday," the new arrival informed Denis. "I don't have it with me, more's the pity. Before you leave tonight, let's make an appointment to meet up before you go back to the States. I would be proud if you'd autograph my copy."

Sara Newland-Attwood made certain Denis was looking at her before she rolled her eyes.

He snickered. That gained him another smile from the enigmatic author and columnist.

The principals were guided to the stage by Douglas Newman. Denis experienced disappointment. Because it was a radio broadcast, there was no grand, pretentious set. There were five folding chairs placed around two long, folding, church-bazar tables. Tommy Dunn was seated at the end of one table facing Denis who would occupy the chair on the other end. Sara Newland-Attwood was located between Tommy and Douglas. Clive sat between Douglas and Denis on the other side. There was a mounted microphone and a clear glass tumbler filled with water at each station. The sound engineer got a sound check from everyone.

"I'm little Tommy Dunn, and I ain't havin' no fun."

"Sara Newland-Attwood and, in this crowd, I am My Royal Highness."

"I'm Douglas Newman, and I'm going to have my hands full this afternoon."

"I'm Clive Martin, and I don't get paid enough to be seen with this lot."

"I'm Denis Wagner, and I haven't anything witty to say."

The sound engineer must have been very good. This was all he needed to adjust his equipment.

Moments later, the audience filed in. It cost nothing to get in, but it wasn't raining outside. Had it been, security would be required to turn people away. As it was, many of the two-hundred and fifty seats remained empty.

Douglas stood and welcomed the audience. He introduced the panel individually. The audience offered profound applause for the "stars." Denis rated only a tepid response. He realized that as a non-performing American, there was no enthusiasm for his presence.

A minute or so later, Douglas got his cue. Music came up from speakers strategically deployed around the auditorium. The host introduced the program, himself, and the panel. He quickly explained the rules and - well, let the games begin!

"We will begin with you, Tommy Dunn. The first topic is France. Would you be so kind to tell us about France for ninety seconds? Start – now."

Tommy Dunn, who owned a summer home in the south of France, began rattling off a tale *in French*. After several seconds, Clive pressed his buzzer.

"Clive Martin, you challenge. On what grounds?"

"Well – I know that this is being heard all over the world on the BBC *WORLD* Service. Many listeners learn English from this program. Wouldn't it be courteous to speak it?"

Douglas pondered this conundrum for a moment.

"I am inclined to agree. Clive, you have the subject of France. Begin now."

Clive began rattling off a rapid-fire narrative – in French.

"Tommy, you challenged."

"Same challenge. Same grounds."

"Correct. You have regained the subject with seventy-eight seconds remaining."

The audience laughed heartily. They expected comedians to be funny. The antics of these celebrated wits got the program off to a good start. Denis felt the sweat inching its way down his spine. He was not a funny man. He prayed that, when his turn came, he could speak without a quiver in his voice.

Tommy led with two points to one to none to none after the first speaker.

"Sara Newland-Attwood, you are the next to tell us something about France."

There were two early challenges. Tommy and Clive both opted for facetious and nuisance challenges, partly for laughs and partly to gain points for their female opponent. After these interruptions, Sara Newland-Attwood related how, in 1936, she was arrested by Parisian police for wearing trousers in a social club. After her time expired, gaining an additional point, there was a brief inquisition.

"Yes, it is the absolute truth," she insisted. "There was, at the time, a city ordinance that women were prohibited from wearing anything other than skirts and dresses."

"And you didn't know that?" Tommy asked, eagerly.

"I didn't," she replied. "Well, not the *first* time."

That fetched a healthy laugh from the audience.

"There were others?" Douglas prodded.

The woman's smile beamed.

"Before I left the city, the police and I were jolly good friends. I intended to make a statement. I did."

There followed a round of applause.

Clive was next. He liked to go to the Riviera when he could get away, but preferred Monaco. He got buzzed for this; the topic was France not Monaco. Tommy got the subject, started speaking French again, and Clive buzzed to get the topic back.

Denis paid little attention to the humorous byplay. He was sweating bullets. He'd be next, and what he knew of France was only slightly more than he knew about nuclear physics.

"We finish up with this round with Denis Wagner," Douglas announced, like the voice of doom. "Denis, what can you tell us about France? Beginning – now!"

"I was in France only once," he began, hoping someone would buzz him. "I didn't have a passport. You see, I escaped the draft because of a physical condition that I do not care to mention here."

Tommy held up the buzzer. For a fleeting moment, Denis thought he was about to gain a reprieve. Inexplicably, however, Tommy refused to challenge. Douglas shot Tommy a warning glance. Denis Wagner was a *Remember When* virgin. Newbies, traditionally, are accorded special treatment.

"I didn't have a passport. Well, in a manner of speaking, I did; it was a press credential."

He told of the night when he was more afraid than he had ever been. He used the phrase "inky darkness" attempting to draw a challenge for plagiarism or, failing that, triteness. Unfortunately, he was forced to drone on.

As Denis described his brief encounter with a wounded woman correspondent, Sara Newland-Attwood's eyes grew large. She'd been casting furtive glances at him since they settled in behind their respective mics. Suddenly, she was staring directly at him. There was nothing furtive about it.

Buzz

Even the audience appeared stunned. Douglas had to consult the light display in front of him to see who had buzzed.

"Sara Newland-Attwood, you challenged."

"Keep your pants on, woman!" Clive bellowed.

The audience laughed. Well, the comedian expected no less. However, there was an edge in his voice. He wanted to hear Wagner's story. He was slightly peeved at the interruption.

"I know this story," Sara Newland-Attwood announced.

"You know this story?" Douglass asked incredulously. "How do you know this story?"

"Care to see the scar on my leg?" she countered.

"That – that was you?" Denis asked in genuine astonishment.

"I'm certain it must have been," she replied.

There was a profound silence – deadly poison for a radio show. Douglas was used to leaping into the void. This time, he did not. He was hypnotized by the surprised expressions on the faces of the principals.

"I beg your indulgence," she continued.

It wasn't clear if she was addressing the program's moderator or the American guest panelist.

"On that stressful evening, I let slip a few injudicious remarks about William Russell that I would not care to have repeated."

"So," Denis began with false bravado. "Did you survive that night? I've often wondered."

Douglas had never seen Sara Newland-Attwood at a loss for words. Not, that is, until that moment. She cleared her throat while groping for a reply.

"My friends seem to think so."

The comment fell as flat as the proverbial pancake. Neither Clive nor Tommy could manufacture a laugh, genuine or otherwise.

It was Wagner's turn to clear his throat.

"If I had known your identity, I'd have been much less abrupt."

"We never did introduce ourselves," she replied. "That was thoughtless of me."

"I'm Denis Wagner, by the way."

"Pleased to make your acquaintance, Mr. Wagner. I'm Sara Newland-Attwood, the only woman stupid enough to be running around during a shelling. Everybody else had the presence of mind to dive for cover. My daughter is meeting me after the show. I would like very much for you to meet her."

"That's done then," Douglas interrupted. "Now, where the hell were we?"

He looked first at those sharing the stage with him. Then, he appealed to the audience.

"In all the years I've hosted this show, I've never gotten lost."

Sara Newland-Attwood regained her regal demeanor enough to come to his aid.

"Mr. Wagner was telling us about France," she prompted. "He still has the subject. I'd much appreciate it if he would tell us something *else* about France."

"I don't know anything else," Denis admitted.

Tommy buzzed.

"If he's finished, I'll have another go."

"A correct challenge, Tommy. You have twenty-two seconds remaining on France."

Yet Another "Most" Unforgettable Character

by Spencer Reed

Before I begin, allow me to state that nobody with the intelligence of a newt would ever go on record as considering Paisley Newland-Attwood a "character." She is a *force.* Her mother, of course, is the famous British journalist and horticulturist. How or why Paisley came to America has never been disclosed by her or anyone in her family. How or why she came to work for us is similarly classified.

I suspect she simply came to work one morning, and nobody had the gumption to escort her out.

I am but one of a team of overworked and underpaid "correspondents" who slave in the second tier of *The Kinderhook*, a monthly journal containing literary and theatrical reviews, (apolitical) social commentaries and observations. We have two features: a short story or poem by unknown (as yet) authors and a reprint of an article of, at least, fifty-years of age. We've even print cartoons on occasion.

The Kinderhook was the brainchild of Walter Able, a New York snob who decided that *The North American Review* needed competition. Since its appearance in 1898, *The Kinderhook* left New York and found homes in Chicago, and Lawrence, Kansas before creating a chaotic work environment in Nashville. The big shots work upstairs, next to the editors. We (there are eight or us) provide fillers and blurbs, mostly. Once in a great while, we pass along an feature that just "might" get included in an upcoming issue. If we succeed, we get a nice bonus. If not, we must settle for the base salary which, I assure you, is *base.* Our two greatest hopes are being promoted to the floor above or finding a better-paying billet elsewhere.

Paisley has a cubicle on our floor, but she spends considerable time with the "higher ups." She's a copy editor, researcher, grammarian, and a repository of information that, very nearly, renders the internet useless.

She has a modest figure which she keeps well togged. Her hair is midnight black and well-tended. Most remarkably, she never talks about herself. What we know comes from little scraps of information people pick up in pursuit of something else. When one finds information about Paisley, it often sounds spurious. This leads to investigations (only on our own time).

The following is a sample:

She earned a degree at seventeen and an advanced degree two years later.

She speaks fluent English, Latin, and Greek both ancient and modern. There are "hints" she speaks, at least two other languages.

She wears contacts when not working.

When working, she wears a pair of owl glasses with ominous black frames that are positively terrifying.

She likes to flirt with the secretaries and female staff, suggesting . . . well . . .

She flirted with me one day over lunch, if that's worth anything.

To repeat, Paisley just appeared one day. She was a curiosity, but no one called her out. Gradually, we learned that she was reviewing all the copy before it was sent upstairs. When she found a grammatical, spelling, or informational error, she'd send a typed memo with the returned material. At first, we took umbrage. Ultimately, however, we agreed that it was better for Paisley to admonish us rather than the suits who signed our checks.

I found myself following her as she flitted about. She was very pretty, though, as previously noted, her figure was not one to arouse envy. Paisley was a good place to rest my eyes, but I had no congress with her (my submissions, thus far, have not been returned with a sharp memo).

One day, however, I discovered that there was more to Paisley than a pretty face and fright-night glasses.

"Paisley," Owen Richards, a cellmate, was bold enough to hail her as she passed by.

She stopped and turned to hear.

"What's the difference between *lama* and *llama*?"

He spelled them out.

"There's an *l* of a difference," she replied, deadpan and glaring at a dictionary within Owen's reach.

"I'm serious," he protested.

She pondered for a moment. She, perhaps, sensed she was being tested. Until she knew for certain, she'd go along.

"*Lama,* one *l*, is a high Buddhist priest – well, I'm not certain the Buddhists have priests, but they do have *enlightened* teachers. *Llama* is a South American dromedary – or of the dromedary family."

Some minutes later, I watched as Owen reached for the dictionary. He quickly settled his mind, or so I thought. Seconds later, he leaned back in his chair and smirked at his monitor.

"Did she pass?" I asked, quietly.

"Spot on, except for the *dromedary.* They have humps on their backs. Llamas don't have humps."

"Still the camel family though?"

Inexplicably, I found myself coming to Paisley's defense.

"Yeah," he sighed.

He got back to work, and I followed suit.

An hour later, Owen snorted and tittered.

"What?" I asked, hoping he'd fetched a literary pearl.

"*There's an l of a difference,*" he repeated.

I joined in this moment of mirth. The comment was funny. The humor was magnified by Paisley's dead-pan delivery.

Paisley is no fool. She knew she was being tested. I doubt she minded, but business hours were, for Paisley, *business* hours. She resented intrusions. When she spoke, she was brief and on topic. She did not resort to small talk.

During lunch and, I presume, after hours, she let her hair down. Despite her copious cerebral resources, her Oxbridge education, and her aristocratic heritage, Paisley Newland-Atwood was a young girl, not at all different from many other young girls. She could be as banal and capricious as anyone.

We ate in herds. Normally, there were three to six people together on any given day. We had our pick of eight acceptable food choices within easy walking distance of the office. For special occasions, a few might hail a cab or catch a bus to a proper sit-down establishment. Normally, however, Paisley contented herself with a salad or sandwich in the company of others so inclined.

"Let's not talk shop," she frequently admonished if anyone tried to quiz her on grammar or vocabulary. This was infuriating. When I asked a question, I required instant gratification. Paisley, however, would not allow business to interfere with her "free time."

She laughed at inane jokes and puns. Hers was the shoulder everyone was welcome to cry on. The enjoyment she obtained by listening to our insipid, day-to-day adventures and misadventures was obvious; her probing brown eyes (devoid of her fright spectacles) danced and sparkled at our every word. Delightfully, Paisley was the repository of no few "naughty" stories – nothing truly lurid, but certainly not the sort of material one would launch at university during high table.

At lunch, she was ever gay and outgoing. Either she was flirting with everyone, or she was flirting with no one. I'm not bold enough to pass judgement either way.

Back at the office, she reverted to her stone-faced demeanor. If she asked a question, she expected a brief, non-evasive answer. If she fielded a question, she responded with pity exactitude. She wouldn't tolerate anyone introducing a question or request with a lengthy speech.

"I don't care *why* you want it," she'd interrupt. "Tell me *what* you want."

As she reviewed all our electronic and printed material before sending it on, the *why* of anything was certain to manifest itself.

I became paranoid whenever she approached me. Her lunch-time persona never appeared in the workplace.

"Will you, *please*, learn the proper use of the semi-colon," she snapped.

"You authored a beautiful, poetic, adjective clause, Spence," she barked at me one morning. "Pity it doesn't modify anything."

I was horrified.

"When did I do that?"

"The fish-market thing."

"Where?"

As I related before, I wanted instant answers.

"Are you a dunce?" she demanded. "It should be obvious. Give proofing your work a try."

That had me boiling. However, when I found this egregious error, I was truly ashamed not to have noticed it.

She called my clause *poetic*. Paisley Newland-Attwood said that about *my* writing!

On a particularly playful day, I composed – in a matter of minutes – a nice little poem of twelve lines in place of a short, literary review. I was very proud of it. I was eager to follow Paisley to lunch that day and see if I couldn't get a plaudit or two.

I didn't make it.

Paisley came by my station and placed my printout copy in front of me.

"Extremely clever, Spence," she said. "Pity, it doesn't scan."

Damn! I'm a journeyman hack, not a poet. I thought cleverness trumped poetic exactitude.

I held my tongue, however. Paisley did not argue or debate. My poem had to go through her to get to the suits. Clarence Darrow couldn't move her. I stood no chance.

"She collects words, you know."

This observation came about from a fellow slave while we were eating our sack lunch. I eyed her curiously. I was aware of the antecedent of that give-away pronoun. When Paisley was not lurking, she featured in many intra-office conversations.

"I'm not surprised," I responded. "I should have figured that out for myself."

"If any word comes from a Latin or Greek root, she can rip off a definition – even if it doesn't make any sense."

I filed that away. I wondered what other languages "she" studied. It never occurred to me that Paisley delved into ancient tongues. However, if one's business is words, a knowledge of our classical roots would be a huge advantage. That she "collected" words – well, that fit right in with her mysterious and somewhat eccentric personality.

From that day forward, I made a point to resurrect words which had fallen out of use. Instead of saying "hello" or "good morning" when I spied Paisley, I would launch my mummified word. Many times, she was cognizant of its existence. However, when I hit upon an unfamiliar gem, she added it, and its definition, to the lexicon that resided inside her capacious cranium. On these rare occasions, she would reward me with a smile and a sincere "thank you."

One day, I failed to dredge an archaic verb or noun. I stole into the work bay like a thief to avoid greeting her or being detected. I knew I'd not get away with it, but . . .

During the morning (unofficial) coffee break, I remained on station. I was startled by a silent figure looming over my left shoulder. Like an Apache warrior or cheap underwear, Paisley can creep up on the unsuspecting. She said nothing as my panicked brain scrambled to retrieve something.

"Jobation," I squeaked.

Paisley pursed her lips into a display of disappointment. She knew the word; she knew the definition; she knew why I'd been avoiding her. However, she patted me on the shoulder before moving away. I accepted her gesture as recognition of my feeble attempt, but my heart bled. I'd disappointed her.

Kinderhook offered up a puzzler from time to time. In pre-internet days, this was a regular feature. When readers need only search the internet, the "puzzler" was reduced to infrequent, cameo appearances. The editors, however, encouraged staff to submit potential head-scratchers. Nearly all were rejected.

One evening, I fought ennui by settling in with a clipboard and a dictionary. After three hours, I produced a thirty-two-word quatrain.

What the hell?

I copied it onto my word processor and sent it to the printer in Paisley's "zone."

(No one on our floor was allowed an office. Those were reserved for the upstairs royalty.)

Paisley was prowling elsewhere when I retrieved my submission. I thought it best to test it before being told it "doesn't scan."

Owen examined it for longer than was prudent. Paisley, ever ready to pounce on slackers, was standing at his station with her forehead knitted in disapproval. Owen defended himself by offering up my poem as a gesture of peace.

"I can't find the anomaly," he stated, apologetically.

My stomach knotted.

Paisley frowned.

Paisley read.

Beads of sweat broke out on my brow.

"It isn't very good."

She had to say that, as if I wasn't aware of my limitations as a poet. Remarkably, she patiently continued her examination. Finally, her smile beamed.

"This is very clever," she congratulated. "I'm taking this upstairs myself."

Were it anyone else, I'd have arrested her long enough to sign my name on the printout. Paisley, however, was not anyone else. I was confident I'd get credit.

Owen eyed my carefully as Paisley retired with long, quick strides.

"Thirty-two words," I informed him. "Only one vowel."

He couldn't grasp it at first. He'd read it. There were several vowels, else there'd have been no coherent words. Gradually, he realized.

"I want to see that again," he announced.

"Later, junior. We'd better be doing something when Nurse Ratchet returns."

She disappeared as mysteriously as she arrived.

Paisley Newland-Attwood lorded over her galley slaves for almost eight months. She was a domineering and harsh mistress on deck. At lunch, however, she was open and honest – and delightful. She plied us with short, riveting anecdotes. Many of these centered around her remarkable mother. All of them sparkled with erudite diction and superb metaphors. She could be witty and have us roaring; she could be sullen and have us in tears. Amazingly, she did not dominate our lunchtime symposia; it merely seemed so in retrospect. She was an alert listener.

I often wondered if she merely humored us. Compared with her narratives, our tales were littered with blue-collar language and events. Nevertheless, Paisley appeared to hang on our every word. She often asked cogent questions.

After she disappeared, we were universal in rejecting the early rumors of Paisley the flirt.

We, mistakenly, judged her by our cultural backgrounds and experiences. Paisley, however, was – well, Paisley. She exists in a unique, intellectual, and ethereal community which is shared by very few.

I wish I could experience that existence – if only for a short time.

The End of the End

Note: Dorothy L. Sayers penned an excellent mystery set in the Fen Country. However, with the solution came the novel's end, I was disappointed. Many interesting questions and facets of the people involved were left unexplored. I have amended Miss Sayers's plot to suit my own purposes.

Earl Main was the latest incarnation of the first manor house on the Fens. No earl ever lived there. The origin of the name remains obscure, and the locals seldom referred to it as anything other than "The Hall." Once it was a showplace. It boasted three or four fishponds, a dovecot, and a mill. As with most medieval residences, it was located near the church which was wisely situated on the highest ground for many miles. When the area was cross-diked and drained, the fishponds disappeared, and the resulting arable land was rented out to the "peasantry."

Jane Wentworth studied the house from the dirt track linking the dispersed settlement of East Ogle with the commercial center of Near Holland. Her sad eyes examined the decaying facade of the stately home, her birthplace. It lingered in need of repair for some while, but . . .

Before her birth there were expansive gardens. What little remained was overgrown. The shrubbery, once surrounding the edifice was poorly tended. There were gaping holes in the once pristine hedge.

Well, Miss Jane mused, there'd soon be money enough for refurbishing.

Miss Jane was, or will be once she comes of age, a wealthy woman. She didn't know about money or its proper dispersal. She wasn't sure she wanted to remain in the house. Should she decide to take the money and reside in Paris or Rome . . .

Miss Jane sighed.

"There be money enough to send you to Oxford," her father announced. "Girls don't seem to cost very much there."

These were, nearly, his last words – to her, at least.

Daddy returned from the war broken in body and spirit. Jane arrived three months after Daddy was crippled in the trenches. Mum, the rock of the family, tended young Jane while keeping her invalid husband alive when both service doctors and Dr. Higgs, the village physician, held out little hope. Mummy ran the house on his behalf. After she succumbed to the Spanish Influenza, Daddy's days were numbered. He knew it. He didn't arrange for her stone. When he passed four months later, he left instructions to be buried in the same grave.

Miss Jane was returning from a visit to the church cemetery. She inspected the manor house and pondered.

Mrs. Moore, a ghastly woman, – even Daddy couldn't stand her – had given notice. She had family problems of her own. After "the master's" death, Mrs. Moore had little reason to remain. She spent most of her time in and near the growlery where Jane's father spent his days. She kept the room clean though the wall hangings and draperies were so old and dreary that dusting and sweeping hardly made a dent in the gloom. "Miss Jane" spent most of her time in her room or the library and tidied up after herself. She would spend an hour or two a day in the growlery with Daddy to spell Mrs. Moore.

Jane was tempted to examine the drawing room. It was once the showplace of the house, but she'd not been there for months. It was the drawing room where visitors gathered for tea and a chat. With Mummy's passing, society ended. Doubtless, Mrs. Moore left it pristine. The memories would crowd Jane, so she eschewed it.

She sighed again.

The house was so empty. Other than wallowing in sorrow or pondering the future of the "manor" (or her own), she'd no reason to enter. She contemplated imponderables elsewhere.

She had a bike, but opted to walk down the lane, past the church, and onto the public house. There she could enjoy a snack, a glass of shandy, and, perhaps, a chin wag. It was a bit early, but she might discover some itinerant with whom she could exchange a word or two. If not, she'd have to endure Mr. Thorne's review of recent events or, worse, Mrs. Thorne and layer after layer of grieving over Jane's loss or layer upon layer of sympathy for Jane herself.

Mrs. Thorne was persnickety about women in a public house. Her husband, many villagers and, even, the vicar reminded her that a "refined" woman could patronize a public house without inviting scandal (all within the embrace of the parish boundaries were considered *refined*). The landlord's wife relented only so much: a woman must seat herself at the small table furthest from the fire and nearest the window. She was allowed a plate of food and a shandy, but loitering was discouraged.

Mrs. Thorpe was certain to have a cow when Jane entered and ordered tea and jam. The woman would cringe over the presence of an aristocratic woman in her establishment. That, alone, pricked Jane on.

Mr. Thorpe had more liberal (modern) views. He knew the war had changed everything, society especially. There was no call to retain this no-ladies-allowed tosh. He best reflected local opinion about the demise of aristocratic manners and airs. For him, Jane was one more shinning face in the village – intelligent, polite, and nominally cheerful.

"There's a great silver lining, however," he said to her on the way to church one Sunday. "Them jewels was recovered. They're yours, ain't no doubt. You grandfather paid the duchess their full value. You be a wealthy woman in two years, Lady Jane."

Jane bristled over "Lady." She reminded the balding Mr. Thorpe that she'd managed quite well as *Miss Jane.* The death of her parents and the recovery of the jewels couldn't make her a *lady* any more than great wealth would make Mr. Thone anything more than the village publican. How is it that she, the last surviving member of the local aristocracy, realized that the aristocracy, as a national institution, was dead? The war killed it. Those of the nobility who survived the slaughter were confronted by a dearth of labor. Just as it was after the Black Death, the great, high, mucky-mucks were forced to compete with agriculture, trades, and manufacturing for servants to serve, butlers to butle, and footmen to tend to visitors (of which there'd be precious few).

Just prior to the war, when Mummy and Daddy were married – when the jewels were stolen – there were fourteen "on staff" (counting the under gardeners). By war's end, there was only Mrs. Moore who lived with her own family and *not* at The Hall.

In the spring of 1914, Mummy and Daddy were joined in the church. The reception was held "up the manor." Among the guests were two lords, a marquis, and *the* duchess, an elderly curmudgeon who was the last of her line. This woman had more pride than she'd earned and was as vain as a medieval monarch. Whenever she appeared in public, she made certain to be draped in jewels. Jane never learned why she was an invited guest. The duchess was a forbidden subject until a few months prior when the newspaper vultures dug up the bodies.

The duchess was a "bloody fool." That much Jane knew from overhearing her father in congress with the local vicar one afternoon. Jane was shocked that her darling father would use such language, but to use it when addressing clergy . . . !

"A wealthy woman parading about in all those jewels; jewels that were not insured! She should have been spanked."

At this juncture, the young (ten or eleven years old) Jane fled to protect her "virgin" ears. It was two days before she could renew a speaking acquaintance with her father.

Well, he was right. The jewels had no business being flouted before all and sundry without being insured. The duchess was repeatedly warned that there were thieves aplenty, even on the Fens.

"I do not associate with loathsome people," she scolded.

Nevertheless, her fortune in jewels was stolen in Grandpapa's home by Grandpapa's butler, and Grandpapa insisted on making full restitution. As a result, Jane, her sainted mother, and darling papa returned from their honeymoon as virtual paupers. Their only income was the annual rents of hardy locals who lived and farmed on Wentworth land. Darling Papa made a few additional pounds by completing a monograph of his regiment's exploits during the war. He suffered anew by reliving and putting into words the horrors he'd witnessed.

James Lee, Grandpapa's senior servant, could not resist taking the jewels. He conspired with an underworld figure and used his position of trust to "relieve" the duchess of her pelf. It was botched. Both Lee and his accomplice were captured in a matter of hours. However, the jewels were never recovered.

James was sentenced to six years labor. His accomplice, a repeat offender, received a stiffer sentence. James Lee murdered a warder, escaped, murdered a hiker, exchanged clothes, and managed to escape to France. Amid the chaos of the war, he melded into a farm community, not very unlike East Ogle. He married, started a family, and settled down to life as a French farmer.

Several months after Lee's escape, a body was discovered in a wood. As it wore prison clothes, and no other trace of Lee was ever found, the law was satisfied. When the former fugitive learned of his "death," he returned to England to retrieve some "property," or so he told his "wife."

His greed overpowered his intelligence. True, he was sneaking around the church in the dark, but he should have realized that electricity had been introduced in his absence. The coroner ruled that the man died of electrocution, but the body was so mangled and battered that identification was impossible. He was quietly buried in a pauper's grave on the south side (nearest the floodplain) of the church.

Nearly a year later, the mystery was resolved.

Betty Newman was a very young parlor maid at the manor. James Lee took a fancy to her. They were married two years before the heist. Poor Betty was rumored to be a co-conspirator, but it was clear she knew nothing of the plot. Her husband used her to find out where the duchess hid her adornments, but she was, otherwise, guiltless. Betty, however, showed up at the trial, convinced her husband was innocent. By the time the judge handed down sentence, even the "grieving wife" had to agree that her husband was a common thief. A prisoner of tradition, Betty never considered divorce.

"*For better or worse*," she moaned before bursting into tears.

She knew not what would happen when James was released. She was not looking forward to his return. After his escape, she was frightened at every nocturnal sound – fearing her husband would force her to hide and care for him.

As she enjoyed her bread and jam, Jane pretended to enjoy her tea. Though Mrs. Thorpe was not in evidence, she may have set aside coarse leaves to discourage any women patrons. Perhaps, the late duchess would have instigated a row. However, she would never set foot in such a "loathsome establishment" as a country inn. Jane, raised on plebian rations, refused to complain of the substandard tea. Mr. Thorpe was a kindly gentleman; nothing would be served by lodging a complaint.

There were only three other patrons at that time of day. Miss Jane's appearance prompted the trio, and Mr. Thorpe, to dissect, yet again, the tragic tale of the purloined jewels. Miss Jane refrained from entering in. Brushing aside the certainty that she had naught to contribute, it wasn't her place (as a young *lady*) to impose upon "man talk."

The inquest, at first, wished to establish the cause of death so the disfigured corpse could be planted as soon as possible. However, the coroner was equally anxious to identify the body for the purpose of proper identification. The man wore the clothes of an Englishman, but his underneaths were of French manufacture. This anomaly cocked many an eyebrow and added to the thrill of the mystery.

Medical evidence concluded that the man died from "sustaining a severe electrical discharge." After his death – "some while after death" – the body was moved and beaten mercilessly.

"Someone, did not want this man identified." Inspector Addison from Near Holland testified. "His face was, virtually, obliterated."

The coroner cleared his throat as he made a note on the thick foolscap before him.

"Did you take fingerprints?" he asked.

"As a matter of routine," Addison replied. "We hadn't much hope, understand. We were fooled into believing the deceased was French. The prints were forwarded to Scotland Yard. They could, then, forward to the *Sûreté*."

"That may take some while," the coroner frowned.

"Not at all, sir. We heard back the following afternoon. The man was not French. He was English. His name was James Lee . . ."

What followed can best be described as cacophony and confusion. Order was restored, eventually. The inspector interviewed Tom and Betty Wythe for some while. His interest was aroused when, a few days after the discovery of the body, Tom, Betty, and their two children, Mildred (8) and Ellen (4), disappeared suddenly. They left no word. They returned after eighteen days, morose and aloof. They hardly spoke to anyone. When the larder emptied, they sent little Milly to market with a shopping basket half her size. The frightened little girl didn't offer any explanations. She said, only, that her parents were not happy.

Inspector Briggs might not have been as adroit or experienced as the Scotland Yard "experts," but he untangled the mystery immediately.

When the inquest resumed, he had a man stay with Betty and the children in their cottage when Tom was called as a witness. He, correctly, reasoned that Tom would be less inhibited if his wife was not present.

The coroner had little opportunity to ask questions. Tom wanted to make a clean breast of things and related his actions in stark detail.

He discovered the body early one morning. He looked out the kitchen window the night before and noticed a light near the church. Someone had a torch. He was curious, but not enough to investigate. When he rose to feed the horse and milk the cow, he opted to stroll over to the church and have a quick look.

Tom discovered the body.

"Quite dead, he was," he gulped. "I turns him over and – it gave me the fright of my life!"

"Did you recognize this unfortunate man?" the coroner prompted.

"Of course! It was like a visit from the grave. It was James Lee – older and bulkier, but it was he, and no mistake. Well, I was scared – I never been so scared in my life. And angry. I was so angry! This miserable creature – what he did to Betty, and – and – well, I takes me shovel and bashed him like a crazy man! I hated him for scaring me out of my wits and for what he did to Betty – and I, I just wanted to beat him until I hadn't any strength left . . ."

"You moved the body?"

"Yes, sir. I – I wanted to get him away from the church, you see. A man like that, has no business bein' there."

"Where did you get the shovel?"

"It be mine. I took it with me – in case I found someone that was up to no good."

There followed a long lapse during which Tom relived the events of that morning. He was breathing heavily and wringing his hands. The coroner felt it best to let him gather his wits before pressing on.

"What then?" he prompted at last.

"I – I was thinkin' 'bout Betty and the little uns. That bloody James! We thought he was dead. We got married all them years ago, then – we went through some very tough times together. Then, suddenly to realize that we was never married – I mean – well, I had to tell her. There was no way I couldn't."

"So, you took her away."

"Yes, sir. We went to Norwich and . . ."

"Inspector, will you be bringing charges against this man?"

The inspector rose from behind the desk assigned him.

"Failure to report a death is a punishable," he mused. "Tampering with, and destruction of evidence . . . However, there are extenuating circumstances. To be blunt, I must file charges, but I've no wish to see him punished."

"Quite so," the coroner nodded. "And Mrs. Wythe?"

"I'm satisfied she had no part in this, before or after the fact."

"And a wife cannot testify against her husband," the aging medical examiner added.

"Just so, sir. To my way of thinking, she is the most aggrieved party in this matter."

So that's how it was. "This matter" shook the tiny community. Even those who whispered doubts and faint accusations against Betty in the past underwent a change of heart. Communal feeling was unanimous in support of the woman. Tom, however, was not *exactly* shunned, but no one was comfortable with his brutal beating of a dead man – even a thief and bigamist. He preferred to keep on the farm or in the family cottage. Betty was tasked with all commercial and social concerns.

Not unlike other married couples in the village, Tom and Betty had suffered through tough times and thin. They bickered and fought on occasion, but the union was harmonious. Their daughters preferred Betty, as Tom could be rather brusque. He wanted a son. Fate denied him. He didn't take out his frustration on either his wife or his daughters, but felicity never managed to lodge long in the little cottage.

After the inquest, Tom was fined and sentenced to a brief stint in the Near Holland "jug." He spent most of his time as a laborer in and about the community. Betty visited once a week *sans* her children. After a month of good behavior, Tom returned to East Ogle to begin his life as a recluse. This existence ended during a local deluge and flood.

One of the low-elevation farms was in danger. Tom left the house to lend a hand. Stock, feed, residual harvest grain, family and family items were driven, carried or herded to safer ground. Tom slipped and fell under the wheels of a heavy-laden cart and –

Betty took this very hard. She reported how Tom wished he were dead because of the shame he brought upon her and the girls. She was more than understanding. She'd been hurt, deeply, twice. However, she made it clear that she did not blame Tom. He didn't know, any more than Betty knew, that her escaped convict husband was alive. Regardless, Tom couldn't forgive himself. He frequently wished that God would strike him down. Well, perhaps God did, but Betty could not rid herself of the suspicion that Tom took a hand in his own fate.

The police were called out again, and another inquest was convened. Betty Wythe refused to appear. She dictated and signed a statement, but her status as a repeat widow was too overwhelming. She kept the children near or in the care of the vicar's wife. It was three days before she felt human enough to have breakfast.

A young PC was dispatched from Near Holland to oversee a, relatively, pedestrian matter. However, he was the first (and, apparently) the *only* person with any curiosity. What, he wondered, was a thief, murderer, and bigamist doing in or near the church? When not representing the constabulary, he poked around. Eventually, he discovered an anomalous patch of brick on the south wall. Once upon a time, hasty repairs were made.

The vicar consulted a dusty volume in the vestry and discovered that the locals, rather than professionals, patched the wall in 1802. Local lore insisted a cannon ball had damaged the church, but there were no records of any fighting nor any mention of a cannon within seventy miles of East Ogle. Regardless, the repair work was accomplished, though it was decidedly slap-dash.

"We've been meaning to make proper repairs for some while," the vicar mumbled apologetically.

The young policeman made a careful study of the amateurish repair works and, eventually, discovered a lose brick. It was, a university historian announced, late Victorian brick. It matched the bricks used in three Near Holland structures, a house, a stable, and a "necessary." In East Ogle, it was decidedly alone and out of place.

Pricked on by curiosity, the novice PC Collins worried the brick out of its niche, revealing a nice little cache. In the void was discovered a hoard worth, at current market value, near ninety-thousand pounds!

This was Miss Jane's inheritance.

Predictably, upon departing the public house, Jane beheld a harried Betty Wythe. Head bowed and weary, the woman ambulated with short, hesitant steps toward the cottage.

The cottage – not *her* cottage. After Tom Wythe's death, she was certain to be evicted. Tom was a tenant farmer. Much of what he produced went to the landlord. The farm never belonged to The Hall. Had it, Miss Jane would, from sheer decency, allow the remainder of the Wythe clan to remain in place, rent deferred, until proper arrangements could be made. As it was, the landlord was as strapped for funds as was most every farmer on the Fens. He could not allow the Wythe farm to remain fallow. The moment a new tenant was found, Betty and her two daughters would be thrown on the parish, hardly a propitious circumstance.

Betty turned catchpenny. She lent herself out for any work offered, whether she was skilled or not. Meanwhile, her daughters spent most of their time in the vicarage, specifically, that place once the schoolroom when the vicar's children were of tender age. They were looked after and fed by the vicar's saintly wife which eased matters a considerably but left Betty beholding.

Miss Jane had never spoken to either Betty Lee or Betty Wythe. She knew, of course, that Betty was a parlor maid at The Hall prior to the "lean years." For obvious reasons, the families eschewed each other. Miss Jane once exchanged words with young, effervescent Milly (who was too young to know why Wythe and The Hall were mutually exclusive).

Those innocent girls who played games of their own invention and filled the air with excited laughter had transformed into brooding, withdrawn creatures who could not understand why their father was taken from them. They were similarly ignorant as to why their mother was somber and exhausted whenever they saw her, which was infrequently.

Miss Jane was moved. She was the mistress of The Hall. Within several months, she would inherit a fortune. Perhaps, the aristocracy was dead. If so, as the soon-to-be wealthiest person for a hundred or more miles, Jane was presented with a stark opportunity to exercise the trite and seldom-observed concept of *noblesse oblige.*

The heiress quickened her step. Jane was quaking. The people of East Ogle were unanimous in their affection for her, but that was before she became the "mistress of all she surveyed." She'd never made a major decision in her life. People who aren't used to making decisions experience chronic trepidation. Jane was certain she was in the right, but, ultimately, it was not hers to judge.

"Mrs. Wythe," she called upon nearing her objective.

It was rude to call out names from afar save during an emergency. Jane hoped she wouldn't be charged with abusing locally accepted decorum.

The grieving woman lifted her head as if frightened. Her head turned toward Miss Jane. The eyes that beheld her were hollow. Betty Wythe, who had appeared moderately attractive from a distance, resembled a wrinkled old crone. Time and life had treated her ill.

Force of habit directed Betty to turn, stand erect and offer the bob curtsy of a servant.

"May I have a word?"

Jane had no hold over Betty Wythe. She made that clear with her respectful but blunt response.

"I must collect the children, mum."

Mum! That archaic mode of address tore at Jane like an ephemeral whip. It was the equivalent of "Go the hell, *please*."

Jane refused to be either baited or insulted. For the first time in her life, she had hit upon a practical, symbiotic notion. She was proud of herself. She respected her own mind. This was her idea, and a reasonable and sensible one.

"Mrs. Wythe, I leave for university soon. Now that Daddy's gone . . . Mrs. Wythe, would you consider being housekeeper at The Hall while I'm away?"

Betty's bloodshot eyes widened.

"The Hall, mum? Lor' I couldn't possibly go back the The Hall, Miss . . . I – the children, understand . . ."

"Mrs. Moore has given notice," Jane hurried on. "You can bring the children with you. You can live there."

Betty's excitement was genuine, but so was her concern.

"The downstairs can be ever so damp." Betty stated, without a trace of hostility.

"Not counting the guest rooms, there are three bedrooms upstairs – well, one is mine, but you could be quite comfortable, all of you."

Betty was shocked and dazed.

"It's so huge!"

"Mrs. Wythe, unless I'm home, there's no one to cook or clean for. You would dust, of course, but there's no one to wait on nor anyone to clean up after. You'd collect mail, cook your own meals, and make your own beds."

Betty Wythe was weakening.

"I – I don't know, Mum – ah, Miss Jane . . ."

"I'm certain we can have someone come round to tend furnace when needed. When I come home from school, I can fend for myself, as I've done most of my life."

Betty was aware of the myriad of bedclothes and coverings. After shivering through several winters in the Wythe cottage, The Hall constituted a palace.

"I'm on an allowance until I come of age," Jane continued. "I can't pay much, but I do want someone in the house while I'm away. Would you be tempted by three pounds a week."

Betty gasped.

"Three pounds! A week?"

"I'm sorry," Jane began, certain she'd committed a fatal *faux pas*, though she was at a loss to understand what it was. "It's the best I can offer at this time."

"Three pounds! A week! I – we – oh, my husband left us with near three hundred in the bank and – I thought it would all be lost if we – but three pounds – a week! Respects, Miss Jane, but I can't be takin' so much money. I – I wouldn't feel right about that."

Miss Jane took a breath. She certainly did not want to insult the woman, but she thought nearly a third of her allowance was rather paltry just for tending the house.

"Suppose, Mrs. Wythe, I deposit money in your account? You take what you need for yourself and the children. When I come home, we can go over the books and settle things. Is that satisfactory?"

Mrs. Wythe choked and sniffed. Her face contorted. The tears flowed, but she struggled to keep from bawling. She, a former parlor maid and bigamously wed (innocently, as was proven by the authorities), was offered a position in The Hall from which she was banished (guilt through wedlock). She was invited to return as a servant, but one that would live *in the house* and not in the dreary servants' quarters. She fought hard for self-control when she realized the "dreary servants' quarters" were luxurious compared to the cottage she and her second husband shared with their family. Indoor plumbing! What a blessing . . . It was a struggle. Eventually, she bit her lip and looked Miss Jane right in the waist.

"Beg pardon, Lady Jane," she squeaked. "Mightn't my girls have the use of the nursery?"

"Mrs. Wythe, what are nurseries for? If you live there, you may use what you please."

Betty's hands flew to cover her mouth. Her eyes shut tightly, and her body convulsed. Jane was tempted to put a reassuring hand on the poor woman's shoulder but feared it would exacerbate souring emotion rather than quell it.

Twelve quid a month! A room for her and the young girls! Her girls could enjoy the nursery! For that – and the twelve pounds – Betty Wythe could scrub, polish, dust, sweep, and launder until her fingers feel off. She wanted to hug the woman who proposed being her benefactor, but the class chasm remained; she could not allow herself to be so forward.

"There is one condition," Miss Jane injected after Betty's emotions crested a wave.

Betty gathered herself up into an attitude best described as attention – not the military variation, to be certain, but the attitude a servant was expected to present when in the mistress's presence. She was relatively collected.

Here it comes, she thought. She braced herself for the clangor. At this juncture, it would have to be most devastating for her to even consider turning her back on a roof over her head and twelve pounds a month in her purse.

"I need a reliable person to look after the house while I'm away," Miss Jane reminded. "You and your daughters are welcome for as long as you care to stay. However, I warn you: I may be very sharp with you should you call me *Lady* Jane. I can't wear it. I *won't* wear it. That title is reserved for my sainted mother. I am no saint."

"Oh, but you are, Miss," Betty insisted at once.

That attitude, Jane concluded, might undergo revision after the quartet shared the same house for a few weeks. Nevertheless, she felt her first *beau geste* as an heiress and *de facto* leading citizen of East Ogle was a logical extension of her family's honor.

Mark Williams

Tread of Specters

The early seventies is remembered for its violence, disquiet, and a marked uncertainty of purpose. The last of my semester final exams was scratched out on a plywood board in the basement of the administration building. The original venue was under renovation. Builders hurried to erase or replace the worst of a firebombing. The campus "advocates for free speech" concluded that the only way to further their cause was to quash any sentiments they found objectionable.

Mother was shaken. She did not want me to return to school until civility returned to public discourse. Father, as always, had a more immediate remedy.

"Send half of the bastards all the way to China, or all the bastards halfway to China!"

It wasn't just American students that advanced the cause of "fear and trembling." Young people the world over were determined to exercise behavior not endemic in a civilized society. Nevertheless, my parents opted to "have a look at Europe" during a time fraught with unrest. The wisdom of such a journey, at that time, was of little interest to me. I was more anxious to be rid of my war with calculous and my battles with physics. At that juncture, I'd have joined the foreign legion – for the summer months, at least.

As the baby of the family, I had no ties. Greta, my eldest sibling, had aborted her career in physical therapy and was struggling to "re-order" her life. Thus, the four of us set off on my parents' adventure long deferred.

Greta would have felt at home with the Amazons of old. She was the tallest and hardiest of we five children. She was a good six foot (I venture, she was a shade taller, but Greta drew the line at "seventy-two inches.") Her tresses were raven and, since her college days, close cropped in a boyish manner. She was "the brain." As a teen, she fancied a medical degree, but sports interfered. Greta could run like the wind and worked magic with a basketball. As her athletic prowess grew, her dedication to pre-med studies was crowded out.

For three years, she was a trainer at a university best left unidentified. Greta enjoyed her work, but she was allergic to the political "nonsense" (her diction). When she got a nose full, she chucked her job and vowed to become a hermit. Even were it possible, Mother and Father were likely to deny her a moment's peace. Greta compromised by promising to "look around," but not until the European vacation was over.

Greta earned the moniker "Stoneface." She maintained a stoic expression when working or socializing. This was a pity. When she smiled, an activity generally reserved for family, her dimples winked like thousand-watt beacons. I saw those beacons in Luxembourg City when she examined the "neighborhood in the ravine." From our vantage on a bridge connecting the two halves of the city, she looked down at the doll houses far below and imagined what it must be like to live in that quiet recess. In Brussels, I beheld it again when we entered the main square surrounded by the old guild halls.

"Wow!" she gulped upon entering the busy pedestrian center of the city. "Now, there is a town square what is a town square!"

Greta was always rather aloof. As the youngest of five, my sensory receptors were limited to the most pronounced and tactile sensations. When I was in third grade, something happened to Greta. The vivacious and vocal creature of my early life became, suddenly, sober and withdrawn. Mother and Father became positively petulant for a long, long while and we siblings gradually adjusted to the chill of the familial hearth. The cause of this "malady" remains a mystery. I suspect my elder brother knew – or had a good idea. Regardless, I never knew, and I was wise enough not to ask.

It was during my struggles with elementary school that I noticed the change. Greta had once doted on me to the point of annoyance. When she ceased attending me and transformed into the great stone face, I realized how much I enjoyed her attentions, annoying though they were. As the oldest child, she set an example for the rest of us (and an admirable example it was), but hers was not the personality we sought whenever we were giddy, silly, or otherwise enjoying ourselves.

In Europe, however, she remained imposing but less aloof. In fact, she and I became "chums." We would leave our parents loitering in a museum or memorizing shop window displays and enjoy an hour or two examining less tedious exhibits. We loved, for example, listening to the locals chatting merrily away in tongues we couldn't understand. We were hypnotized by eateries where fresh fish and produce were arrayed in open-air sidewalk displays. We enjoyed committing medieval homes and building facades to memory and exchanging observations about the most salient features of each.

I laughed when we encountered the Mannequin Pis. Neither of us were aware of its existence until we just happened by. Greta didn't laugh. She's not a puritan, and she didn't express any verbal objections; however, she was decidedly nonplussed. For a moment, I was tempted to give her a nudge and suggest that she "lighten up." I squelched the idea. Would I be nudging a sister who would accept my gesture as a brotherly tease, or would I be jostling a case of dynamite? I decided not to push my luck.

Mother and Father found Holland enchanting. So did I. Greta – well, she can be a tough read at times. She was decidedly *not* bored, but there were no signs of unbridled felicity either.

Just south of Arnhem, over a light but tasty meal and equally tasty local beer, Greta suggested a side trip.

"I'd like to go to Xanten," she announced, quietly.

Father had served in ETO during the war. He wasn't in the front lines, but he'd seen and heard enough that Germany was declared *terra incognita* in the early stages of our planning.

We had Jews a few branches up Father's family tree. It may have been because of that, or there may have been other considerations. Regardless, Greta's suggestion did not add to the ambiance of the afternoon.

"What's in Xanten?" Father asked, using a peculiar tone.

Greta shrugged.

"I want to go to a town that begins with *X*," she replied. "It sounds so Greek. As it's unlikely I'll ever travel to Greece, this may be as near as I'll get."

Father grunted.

There followed a few minutes of guarded silence.

"I could rent a car," Greta resumed. "I could overnight somewhere, return the rental, catch a train and meet up with you in Rotterdam."

The silence cascaded. I apologize for such a strained statement, but the quiet at our table was positively eerie. It was as if blocks of silence were being stacked, one upon another.

"Would you come, Ripple?"

Ripple, I hastily add, is a nickname. Greta is the only person who calls me that. Others have tried, but I protest so emphatically that no one trespasses a second time. When Greta uses this fatuous title, it's always in the family circle. From her, I take no offense. In this case, I interpreted it as an affirmation of her affection. It was with that understanding that I agreed.

Father said nothing more about the matter. This was his tacit assent. So long as I was Greta's escort, he would not allow his prejudices to interfere. We would reunite in Rotterdam and catch the ferry to England.

Greta was the elder, better driver. Further, it was she who rented the vehicle. There was no question about who'd be driving. My job, navigation, was embarrassingly simple. The road signs were frequent and accurate. I pretended to keep track of our progress, but it was superfluous.

Our border crossing consisted of presenting our passports and answering two, routine questions.

As we neared "X-Town," Greta began showing signs of nervousness. This was disturbing. Greta had a deserved reputation for keeping cool under the most taxing conditions. She never got flustered and her judgement under pressure was a family mainstay.

"Are you okay?"

I never thought I'd ever ask that of Greta.

She grunted.

This was serious. Obviously, Greta was extremely *un*kay! Grunts may be standard equipment for most people, but my sister habitually responds by using precise diction. In a flash, our relaxed pleasure outing transformed into something trepidatious.

The road nestled along a diversion (manmade?) of the Rhine. As we followed the curve of the highway, we found ourselves following an escarpment on Greta's side of the road. Obviously, the cut was made to accommodate the construction of the highway. My sister studied it whenever there was a break in on-coming traffic. Did she expect some mythical Teutonic monster of legend to swoop down upon us? She certainly acted as if she did.

The palms of my hand turned sweaty.

She slowed as we approached a natural drainage. There was a dirt trackway and a trio of farm outbuildings nestled amid the foliage. Abruptly, she braked and swung across the northbound lane to slither onto the trackway. By this juncture, I was on the verge of panic. Greta, a studious driver, was not so cavalier. Something was very wrong!

She threw open her door and exited the vehicle. I followed suit and rushed round the car to her side. She stood erect so every millimeter of her height was in evidence. She did not, however, stand the proverbial *stock still*. She was trembling – not just her hands but her whole body. She looked up the steep slope of the drainage. There was no sign that water frequently escaped the plateau. On the contrary, the trackway and the outbuildings testified that serious runoffs were intermittent and minimal.

Were I a normal human being, and were Greta a "typical" female, I'd have demanded an explanation. Greta eschewed "normal" or "expected" behavior. She oozed with confidence and remained calm in the most trying circumstances. Seeing her, suddenly, exhibiting such bizarre behavior was painful and nerve wracking.

"Up here," she gasped.

Even her voice trembled.

She half climbed and half crawled up the steep slope. I followed. If Greta was injured or experiencing some epileptic seizure, I'd stay close. I'd do anything I could to calm or help her. Until I knew what malady seized her, I'd do nothing more than follow her lead.

We emerged an open plain sloping gently north. There'd been a crop here, wheat probably, but nothing remained save coarse stubble. The soil might be fertile enough, but the surface was dominated by small pebbles and sandy, unprepossessing "dirt" (for want of a more accurate word).

Greta quickly moved a few paces ahead with her faithful hound (me) close on her heels. She groaned. She breathed heavily, choked, and fell to her knees. I was at her side instantly and searching her face. I saw something I never expected to see – ever! Greta was in tears. They flooded down her face in a torrent. She swallowed hard, fought for breath, choked again and let go with a mournful wail.

She turned her head as if seeing me for the first time.

"This is a horrible place. Get me out of here. Fast!"

This was no time to ask questions or debate. I doubt I have ever seen a more placid, innocuous landscape in my life. From my hurried survey, I considered it a low-grade rural scene hardly worth more than a cursory glance – which, under the circumstances, was all it got from us.

I got Greta to her feet and held her close and hurried her back to the slope. We half slid and half bounded back to the car.

"You drive!" Greta snapped.

I obeyed, but my attention was divided. I pulled back to the highway and signaled for a left turn. If I could get her someplace and encourage her to put away some brandy, we could assess the situation further.

"Not that way, fool! Get me out of this country!"

Greta had often used her position as the eldest child to make my younger days a misery. She'd called me "fool" often enough, but not for years. We all looked up to her as a mentor and, for reasons never understood, Greta deferred to me more often than the others. Therefore, I ignored her language and proceeded to accede to her wishes.

By the time we returned to the river estuary, she stopped shaking and returned to a facsimile of her normal self. She reached into the glove box and took out the rental car papers. She shook them at me.

"If anything happens, *I* was driving. Understood?"

"Yes, ma'am."

I never called her that before (or since), but I was so heartened by her return to normalcy that I'd have addressed her as the Queen of Pomerania. My nerves were still taut. After a few minutes, she tilted her head back and gulped for air.

"Let's not mention this to anyone. Understood? No one. Not Mother or Father or . . . or anyone! Kapish?"

I concentrated on my driving. That did not divert me from thinking things through. Greta had given me the heart-stopping fright of my life. What if I hadn't come? What if I hadn't been empty headed enough to struggle up that damned slope?

"Before I agree to anything, I needed assurance this was a *one off*. If you need help –"

"Damn! I don't know what came over me. I felt – I don't know; terror, I guess. It was awful. I – I smelled smoke. I heard screams – terrible, horrible screams, and – and – and – that's all I'll say. That's all I will ever say. See, I'm shaking again just thinking about it."

I swallowed very hard.

"It's your call," I announced. "My lips are sealed. Know this: if you freak out again, I refuse to remain silent."

Greta thought that over for several kilometers.

"I'll settle for that," she decided.

I kept my word. Greta kept her cool. There were no more insanity attacks. Had there been, I'd have heard. However, I never managed to erase that terrible episode from my memory. Periodically, it would visit me at the most inopportune moments. After reliving that frightening episode, I would call Greta at the first opportunity.

"Just wanted to call and find out how you're doing," I'd say.

Greta never let on, but she knew exactly why I was calling. She always assured me that she was "hundred percent." We'd chat for a few minutes and exchange best wishes. Save for family Thanksgivings, we'd remain strangers until the next "vision" prompted another call.

Greta never called me. She'd send me a birthday card without fail and enclose sisterly platitudes, but we drifted apart, both vocationally and geographically.

I went to work for a plastics firm as something of a troubleshooter. I'd track down causes for production blips and blarts, submit recommendations, and follow up during implementation. When an employee was a candidate for promotion, I played devil's advocate. I wasn't particularly good at this task. Unless an employee was incorrigible or short tempered, I would offer only the most timid and insipid objections. I hated checking up on people – especially siblings.

Greta ditched the trainer, physical therapy, and therapist business and devoted her life to animals. She loved quadrupeds, dogs and horses particularly. She sheltered them, trained them, and found them good homes. She didn't make tons of money, but she had hundreds of friends, no few were human.

We exchanged post cards and short, if chatty, missives from time to time. However, I didn't see her again until fourteen years after our aborted foray into Germany. Greta had removed herself to the fertile fields of the rural mid-west where her beloved animals abounded, but modern society (and amenities) did not. Only Mother's succumbing after a decade-long struggle with cancer brought the surviving family members together next.

Greta was cheerful and amiable. We five shared many anecdotes about our lives, prior to leaving the nest. As the eldest, Greta's narrations were the most comprehensive. She and Mother were very close. After Greta's decampment, she either phoned or wrote home every few days. During the service and at the grave side, old Stone Face was as ever, while Father and my three other siblings fought back our tears. I could not help but recall our shared German experience when Greta succumbed to a shocking, if temporary, mental collapse. Of course, I made no mention.

Two more years slid past before I took up Tacitus.

Roman history, for me, is not a passion. On the contrary; on a linear scale, Tacitus would be near the moss and lichen end of the spectrum. I had no excuse to give that damned volume more than a superficial flip through. Read it I did, however, and there were profound sections that made an indelible impression.

Curiosity was pricked.

I began researching. With marked eagerness, I was intrigued by Varus leading three legions into the German hinterland and their slaughter. When there was a sufficient compilation of material, I entered the map room of a nearby university library. An intriguing discovery awaited. The three legions of Varus exited a camp very near – wait for it – modern day Xanten!

I will swear in front of anyone, with my hand on the Holy Bible, that I never once even *hinted* about my sister's emotional collapse all those years prior. Greta never indicated that she suspected me. I had given my word, and she trusted me. Imagine, then, my absolute horror when my wife joined me in my research.

Esther's interest in history can best be measured with negative numbers. Her interest in ancient history is lower still. Nevertheless, she needled me about my sudden passion for haunting university library archives. She didn't believe it at first. Why should she? My historical interest was more than satiated by *Gone with the Wind* and John Wayne westerns. When I failed to explain my motives – indeed, I had none – Esther became a pain in the – uhm – *neck*.

She started picking through the copy of Tacitus I obtained via inter-library loan. Our local librarian, doubtless, thought I was either a mental case or a deliberate irritant. Regardless, I was called one rainy afternoon when a copy arrived from the state library. It was one of those editions with Latin on one page and the English translation on the facing page. Since placing my order, I'd found out what I wanted from secondary sources nearer at hand. Still, I'd created a minor inconvenience; it would be rude to say I was no longer interested.

It lay on a coffee table for two days before Esther took it up. She'd exchanged words with our younger son and felt a little ancient history would purge her upset. I was making myself a snack, satisfied that Esther would join me once she realized the volume contained no illustrations.

She never showed.

After finishing up the left-over potato salad, I rinsed off the fork and plate before consigning them to the dishwasher. When I turned the corner to reenter the living room, I experienced a shock. Esther had kicked off her shoes and had drawn her legs up under her. She studied Tacitus while chewing on the thumb of her free hand. Her brow rippled with consternation.

"This is horrible," she moaned.

Instantly, I was back on a German plateau. Esther's troubled voice was disturbingly like Greta's articulation on *that* day.

"They're eating rats and whatever grass is growing in the chinks of the wall."

Her use of the present tense stunned me. I couldn't speak. I'm not certain I could think. It was as if I'd been beaned with a fast ball. I wasn't out, but my cognition was seriously impeded.

"All winter it was like this! They surrendered, finally. The Brac – something or other, made them come out unarmed and were taken away. They are ambushed and slaughtered. A few survivors made it back to the fort . . . The place is torched and the few survivors – This is horrible!"

I managed to get the book from her. I instructed her to watch TV or listen to some music to help wash the narrative out of her head. Esther cries at card tricks, or so it seems. She has instant emotional overload. Her reaction to a narrative centuries old was mild enough, but it put Greta's outburst into sharp focus.

Greta, however, knew nothing of Tacitus – then or now.

The Roman fort near modern Xanten was huge. It was designed to quarter two legions. That required services: grain storage, blacksmiths, mills, bake ovens, water storage, armorers, clerks, tailors, quartermasters – the whole smack. Some officers may have had wives and families; there would be quarters for them. Enlisted men weren't allowed to wed, but they, too, would have "common law" wives living "off post." Of course, there were camp followers who were certain to be nearby. When the siege began, the army post would be very crowded and confused.

I dusted off some of my notes and source materials.

The place was called Vetera. It was refurbished after the loss of Varus and his three legions, but it remained a crude, frontier post. I suppose the top brass thought if anything serious happened, they could pile onto supply transports and go up the Rhine and safety.

The sides of this advanced base were over three thousand feet with a width of over two thousand. It was designed for two legions, but the ramparts were earthen rather than brick. The interior would have been wood save for the headquarters which, normally, was of stone. Accounting for the troops, NCOs, and officers plus granaries, bake ovens, armorers, smiths, quill pushers, carpenters, butchers, leather workers, and other assorted supernumeraries, the seemingly huge complex would be "cozy" at best. There were four gates; each would be guarded. If a squaddie wanted to leave the post to be with his woman, or to hire one, he'd require a pass. If he forgot the password upon returning, his punishment would be memorable.

How did such a huge compound allow itself to be besieged? For most of one year, it was surrounded. Supplies and reinforcements couldn't get in, and the Roman contingent couldn't get out. Wisely, the Germans in revolt waited for the legions to starve themselves into surrender. Disarmed, the skeletal survivors were herded south for miles before their captors fell upon them and slaughtered most of the helpless, famished prisoners. The few who survived the carnage returned to the only place offering pretend safety. Was it already in flames? Alternatively, the Germans waited until the few remaining Romans were once again "locked up" and, only then, burned the place down.

Regardless, the walls were leveled, and the ashes stirred until only scorched earth testified to its existence. When Rome renewed its claim, it constructed a fort nearer the Rhine. What remains of this more recent edifice is now *under* the Rhine. Vetera exists only as a place name. There remains, to the north, an amphitheater, gouged out of the earth. The camp itself has been under the plow for nearly two millennia.

What, I wonder, is Vetera to Greta and Esther? What are Esther and Greta to Vetera?

I'm not into the paranormal or other related pseudo-sciences. Still, two important women in my life were visibly moved by the place. No matter how I arrange my mind, I cannot dispel the disquiet of these two, very different people over a long-vanished world.

I knew the archeologists have picked over the bones. Xanten is a veritable cornucopia of Roman leavings. One can't put a spade in the ground without finding something. Vetera was scoured, of course. There was much evidence of intense burning, but few finds. Presumably, the German rebels picked it clean before vanishing back into the forest. Perhaps, the construction team that erected the smaller, nearby Vetera II, gave it another sweep. Regardless, I went out of my way to get published information of the archelogy reports.

My last ever investigation was in a detailed tome of some thickness. It was in German, but I read the photos and diagrams with ease. In the back, was a large-scale map of the excavated site. I unfolded it and found a survey, topographical map of the area with the walls marked with precision.

I searched for the "drainage" and identified it by the outbuildings and the modern highway. This curious crease must have been carved out after the Romans abandoned the plateau. No Roman engineer would plant a permanent army camp atop such a feature.

My mind slipped back across all those years to that day when a visibly disturbed Greta clawed her way up a steep bank, through bushes and brambles. Once we reached the top, we were in the middle of a long-ago, burned and battered Roman fort! Greta went to pieces. I got the fright of my life.

I leave all speculation to others.

My Pal or Eating Crow

My first dog was Geraldine, a golden cocker. We moved to Oregon when I was five, and Geraldine was hardly a memory, so she must have come when I was very young. My parents insisted that she'd been poisoned. That may or may not be true. I hope she was given away by my parents to a proper home. My sainted grandfather bought me an electric train set for my fourth Christmas and my first bicycle shortly thereafter ("Is he trying to kill the boy?" Mom asked); it is, therefore, my guess that Granddad supplied the dog as well.

Granddad and Dad did not play well together. Our move to Oregon was a manifestation of the friction between them; it was as far from Ohio as our family could get and remain on dry land. Unlike my father, I thought Granddad walked on water. Whenever he visited us, he presented me with a silver dollar.

My second dog was a mutt, born to a mother who roamed the neighborhood. The father was known but to God. Her "owners" (how I loathe that term) were presided over by one of my dad's subordinates on a team tasked with surveying a proposed highway. Their house caught fire one afternoon and the family dog, already heavily laden, was left in our charge since none of the motels allowed pets. She gave birth under the woodshed behind our rented home.

I was tasked with the care and feeding of mommy. When the pups were weaned and their eyes open, the *owners* sought homes for the youngsters. Their task was initiated by "rewarding" me for my service; I got first pick.

Scramble and I got on like a house on fire. Dad, absolutely, would not allow anything but people in the house, so Scramble and I played outside – not a bad arrangement, but we had snow in the winter. I'd take him into the woodshed and provided a place for him.

As he grew up, my interest in him began to slacken. I had so many adventures with the neighbor kids, and dogs were not a part of our games. I recall my dad scolding me for not playing with Scramble anymore.

"He's a big dog, now," I said, because I was a snot-nosed, little jerk who resented my parents butting into my business.

"He's still just a pup," Dad reminded.

That hurt.

The city passed an ordinance that all outside dogs, within incorporation limits, must be restrained. We bought a collar and a twenty-foot chain. Scramble, who loved running, exploring, chasing bugs, birds, and people, felt he was being punished. Head bowed, he dragged his chain over to my mother's clothesline, sat down, and sulked. One would think he'd been beaten. He didn't bark; he didn't whine; he didn't whimper; he didn't respond to anything – he just sat.

My heart broke, but I thought he'd get over it.

Dad, however, couldn't take it. After dinner one evening, he walked out the back door and released Scramble. The dog was instantly joyous and playful. I was stunned – and frightened.

"The dog catcher will get him!" I protested.

Dad said not a word. I could have put Scramble back on the chain, but I hadn't the courage. It was Scramble's expression of sorrow more than fear of my dad that deterred me.

One day, Scramble was gone. He could have been stolen, or run over, or taken to the dog pound. I never knew. I doubt Mom or Dad made any inquiries. He was gone and, until I began writing this, I didn't miss him much.

I hope he got the home and family he deserved.

High school, college, Army, marriage, divorce, living overseas, and a myriad of other "reasons" made a dog far down on my list of priorities. My daughter got a delightful, snow-white pup who was a welcome family member despite the problems he created. Three weeks after he came to us, he became ill. He was taken to vet where he remained a very few days before he died.

It was years before my daughter recovered from that.

After the divorce, my daughter remained with her mother. She lobbied for, and eventually, got a dog – a terrier who, whenever I came to visit, insisted on sleeping in the bed assigned to me. He was a delight until, after three years, he began snapping at my ex-wife.

I chalked it up to either good sense or good taste. However, when he began snapping at my daughter, we reviewed the situation. He started snarling and snapping at me – well, that was serious.

They found a good home for him – a home with professional breeders and trainers who made a show dog of him. He was in several shows around Germany and, I think, placed in a couple of them.

Not long after I settled down in my retirement home, I met Brindle.

It was one morning at the coffee shop and the owner's boyfriend stopped by for a liar exchange with members of the local old-folks coffee club. In the car was an eager creature who looked eagerly through the car window and into the café. I made such a fuss that the dog was brought in for introductions all around.

Ours is a small community in a large county with a tiny population. Informality is the general rule and what the health inspector didn't know wouldn't hurt us.

In comes the friendliest pit bull in the world. He started out as an attack dog, but he wouldn't have it. They tried to make him into a drug sniffing dog, but he wouldn't have that either. My newest friend was lucky enough to be first in line when the trainers advertised.

I would go around the corner and up the street periodically just to say hello to Brindle. He was always happy to see me. In truth, he was happy to see anybody.

Long story short: I was asked to take care of Brindle when the disk golfer and the café lady were out of town. I was happy to do so.

I lived alone in a two story, three-bedroom house. I established a bedroom for my son, should he decide to "drop in." The "guest room" was my library. The moment Brindle arrived, he explored every nook and cranny before claiming my son's bed. He could lay atop it and monitor any activity on our street through the two windows. Every few minutes, he'd come around and want my attention. Once satisfied that I had not abandoned him, he'd return to his lookout station.

I took him for walks. He didn't care to be on a line, but he didn't fuss.

It was zero-dark-thirty when – REVEILLE!

I was snoozing soundly when I heard the most hideous racket. When I peeled myself off the ceiling, I turned on a lamp and found Brindle sitting next to my bed.

What's the matter with you? His puzzled expression conveyed.

I'd never heard a dog shake its ears as he had. I suspect that many soldiers never beheld such a cacophony. Well, I quickly got used to it. During subsequent overnight stays, that hideous noise was reduced to an innocuous little reminder.

I'm awake he seemed to announce. *Now what?*

He was great company and absolutely no trouble whatsoever. I began encouraging my friends to go away for a couple days so I could dog sit.

My daughter has special needs. She's half German, also. Her mother, my ex, thought that Kristina would be more comfortable and could get better support in America. I knew that Kristina and her mother didn't get along well. I wasn't certain that she and I would get along any better, but I was willing to give it a try.

One of Kristina's first American friends was Brindle. They got along well enough that I felt a twinge of jealousy; Kristina got more attention than I.

How would bedtime work out? Brindle's bed was now in use.

There was no trauma, no fuss, no whining. When the lights went out, Bridle lay on the floor next to Kristina's bed. Eventually, they would share the bed. I suspect Kristina encouraged that, but Brindle seldom needed encouragement.

Kristina began lobbying for a dog before she got here. After meeting Brindle, her entreaties intensified. I kept putting her off. Alas, she walked over to see Brindle one day, whereupon Brindle's "daddy" looked on a super-secret local pet site and sent her home with a phone number.

A family was leaving our small, isolated community in Oregon to live in a small, isolated community in Alaska. They were anxious to find homes for their pets, two dogs and two cats.

One of the dogs was a black lab, the dog of choice in our hunting and fishing community. He was on the market for all of eight minutes. The cats and the remaining dog, however, remained.

We called.

We met up at a local motel. Their furniture was sent on ahead. The motel was cheaper than another month's rent. Their departure time was predicated on placing their remaining pets.

Sadie was a sleek, brown pup with a white muzzle and stockings. She was, also, unbelievably shy. She wanted nothing to do with us. Instead, she wanted to play and prance with her owner and his two children. Sadie was on a leash. When Kristina attempted to lead her around, Sadie sniffed at her curiously, but struggled to get back to her proper family.

"This won't work," I advised.

"I want to try," Kristina responded.

She'd fallen in love and refused to see the obvious.

The punk little ten-year-old at my side informed me he couldn't take less than a hundred a fifty balloons for "his" dog. I was ready to recite from the Gospel according to Vengeance, but I promised myself never to use such language in front of my daughter. She was shy as well. Her school days were highlighted by her sneaking from one class to another, clinging to the lockers and walls, thinking she'd be invisible to the other students who scurried through the halls. She had only one or two close friends, and she left them in Germany.

I sang a blue aria as I drove to the nearest ATM for the ransom money.

"I always thought that *Quiche* would be a good name for a dog."

Well, Sadie and her leash got into the back of our car easily enough, but she trembled all the way home. She didn't like it. There were no other dogs and no cats. She was alone with a grump and a young woman who petted her and spoke softly to her.

We were promised that Sadie was house trained. Predictably, the moment she walked into her new home, she pooped on the floor.

The first ten days with *Quiche* are, mercifully, beyond recall. The poor little dog was terrified. It took her some while to warm up to us. She found Kristina tolerable, but she seldom paid any attention to me. When she wasn't pooping in the house, she was hiding – under beds, chairs, anything that provided some shelter from her "torturers."

One evening, she deigned to join us in my bedroom where we were watching some program. Kristina sat on the floor next to Quiche and petted her gently. Eventually, Quiche discovered her tail – it was as long as Quiche's body and impossible to ignore. After a while, she had us in stiches chasing that tail and – from time to time – catching it.

Quiche seemed to delight in our jollity. She no longer made a point of avoiding us. She remained reticent, however, and seldom came to us unless there was the promise of a treat. Gradually, she'd come to us without being bribed.

The inside pooping ceased, but she was not officially ours until I caught her one day on the couch next to Kristina. Her head was in Kristina's lap.

She was home.

Quiche chewed anything and everything. We bought her dog toys and chew toys. Nothing doing. She would chew only on furnishings, clothes, pillows – if she could get her teeth into it, she chewed it. We kept a constant watch, but we unplugged all electrical cords not in use. Thankfully, electrical items were never on Quiche's to-do list.

We walked her over to meet Brindle.

They were best friends at first sight. Sometimes, Bridle got a little annoyed by Quiche's incessant attention, but they frolicked and played until they were stepping on their tongues. Within days, if Kristina or I hid in a closet and just whispered "Brindle," Quiche would have an epileptic seizure and hurry to the front door. She'd turn and look for us, her long tail creating weather systems in the entry way. If we did not set off for a Brindle fix, she'd scold us with blood-curdling howls!

Quiche liked to chase deer. Luckily, we found this out when the fawns were old enough to fend for themselves, but that did not blunt our terror. It's difficult to meet a resident in our small town who doesn't have a dog who got the worst end of a deer encounter. No few have been trampled to death. However, when Quiche spies a deer, she's off to the races! Fast as she is (and she is lightning on four paws), the deer easily outran her once they'd had enough of her attention. When Quiche, finally, gave up the chase, she'd be lost. There were three or four times we were forced to cruise the streets in search of her. Most often, however, we'd find her at Brindle's house, either at the door begging admittance, playing with her best friend inside, or in back frolicking and damaging a neighbor's garden.

We didn't want Quiche to get hurt, so we kept her on a leash if we suspected there were deer in the area. Unfortunately, Quiche didn't like the car. She was always apprehensive about getting in, but we didn't feel comfortable leaving her in the house or the back yard. She's a clever girl and, once she escapes, we expected to find her at Bridle's home. It was a rare occasion, indeed, when she was not there.

My dentist, whom my brother recommended and whom I saw only once a year when I was stationed overseas, is roughly two hundred miles removed from my house. We took Quiche with us once, and she was miserable. She enjoyed being walked around and reading the local doggie newspaper, and she enjoyed making new friends at the dog park. In the car, however, she whined, panted incessantly, or climbed up in the rear window to be both inert and miserable. We would stop periodically, but there was no spring in her step. She didn't want to stay at roadside rests, and she didn't want to get back in that damned car. Further, on sunny days, she risked being cooked in her rear-window refuge.

After this experience, we would leave her with Brindle. Predictably, she pooped on the floor her first overnight. After that first time, however, being with and near Brindle took away her fear and shyness.

Once, we came back and got a report that the dogs had run off. It took an hour in two vehicles to track them down and get them "home."

Kristina and I booked AMTRAK to Chicago to be with my son, his wife and their brand- new daughter for Thanksgiving. The Brindle Boarding House gladly accepted Quiche. She was comfortable there and let us go without a whimper. Brindle was better than us any day!

"Don't you follow Brindle if he runs off again."

"Who said Brindle did the running?"

This challenge changed everything. Quickly, I praised Brindle for watching after our impetuous dog. It made me feel better. If Quiche did bolt, she had a "protector" with powerful jaws to protect her if she caught something she wasn't chasing.

Kristina called once every couple days to inquire about Quiche. Once, she asked to "talk to her." Quiche recognized the voice and wagged her tail, but she was very confused.

Alas, all good things must end.

Brindle became ill, listless, and experienced co-ordination problems. Following several visits to the vet and several tests, the diagnosis was confirmed; Brindle had a brain tumor and, other than medication to ease pain and discomfort, there was nothing to be done. Kristina took Quiche over a few times.

Brindle would wag his bottom and tail meekly, but the playing days were over. Quiche sensed that something was amiss and would lay close to her friend as if to share in the melancholia.

To this day, if one mentions Brindle, Quiche will cease doing whatever she's doing and perk up. She will stare expectantly at whomever uttered the magic word.

Quiche was used to us and, seemingly, accepted us. She remained shy and frightened. She slept under Kristina's bed. If she was nervous, we couldn't get her out from under her "space." Calling didn't help. Offering treats didn't help. If she thought we were leaving in the car, she would cower under the bed until she heard us depart. We found evidence that she would come out while we were away, and she was always happy when we returned. However, to this day, "Quiche and carry" is problematical at best.

Eventually, Kristina decided that we must find another Brindle, a friend who would be a live-in support dog. I was reticent. My heart bled whenever we disappointed Quiche. Getting her to the vet when she suffered from some malady was taxing and exhausting. When we arrived, the provider insisted Quiche get on the scales. For all the fuss and bother, one would think we were forcing her into a nest of vipers. Again, bribery, cajolery, and (our last resort) the good-cop-bad- cop routine had no influence over her.

Brindle's bereaved friends were scouting about for another pet, knowing they would never find a jewel to match their departed. Because they were looking, and because of useful local contacts, they looked on behalf of Kristina as well.

One Friday evening, we got a call.

Brindle's "dad" was a disc-golfer. He and dedicated friends lobbied the town for a disc-golf course and, after three or four years, finally got permission to create one in an existing park. It was a place where dogs, including Brindle and Quiche, enjoyed a good sniff-and-run.

One of the disc-golfers was a dog lover. He, periodically, looked for abandoned dogs. He was looking for a lap dog, but . . .

One day at the kennel, he saw a spirited dog so very excited to see him (or anyone else). The rescue team found him abandoned, starving and dehydrated in a roadside ditch where some ________________________ (expletives deleted) left him – just threw him away like an empty beer bottle. The vet and a team of volunteers put in much time and effort to nurse the guy back to health. Now, however, they had to put him down because no one wanted him.

That was too much. Zack took him, knowing he couldn't give him a proper home. He worked between twelve and fourteen hours a day, so he was desperate to find someone to care for the foundling.

The moment Kristina heard this, she was ready to take him, sight unseen. Cooler heads prevailed. We would meet at the disc-golf course on Saturday morning (the official golf day). If he and Quiche got along – well, first things first.

It took several minutes to entice Quiche outside. If she suspected a car ride, she'd have hidden under the bed, and we'd never make the meeting. However, I had pulled the car out of the garage much earlier, so she was caught unawares. Without a hole or bed to hide in or under, Quiche was trapped. Suspecting another trip to the scales or (worse) an hours-long trip in the rear window, she put up a champion fuss. Eventually, with Kristina in the back seat to comfort her, she relented.

We arrived while the disc contestants were still warming up and awaiting late comers. My heart stopped beating. There was only one dog in evidence.

Frankendog!

He was not much larger than Quiche, but he was substantial. Quiche was sleek and lithe; Frankendog was built like a battleship! He was German shepherd in the front and loadstone Huskey in the back. He was unprepossessing. He looked as if he'd made a career of clearing barrooms of miscreants.

I sat in stunned amazement. Kristina, however, opened the back door. Quiche had only one concern: escape! Before either of us could react, Quiche was in full pursuit of that ugly monster.

I feared the worst. If we were lucky, we could collect the remains of Quiche and hope the vet could put her together again – never to be the same or even a shadow of herself.

Alas, they were best friends from the get-go.

Quiche chased the ungainly beast who, quickly, turned about and chased her. This went on for three or four rounds before they called time out and gave each other the sniff test.

"It looks like they get along," a bearded hulk announced.

It was Zack. He wore a big grin because he had every reason to believe that he'd unloaded an ugly brute. Kristina didn't help. She gave me that *don't-you-dare* glare. I felt like a *Titanic* passenger watching the last lifeboat shove off.

"What's his name?" I asked – croaked, more like.

"Duke."

How original.

Brute would be more apt.

What an ugly mutt! Not only was he bulky and had uglies he hadn't used yet, he shed like his mission was to carpet the county. I calculated he would require elephantine rations. He would poop accordingly.

Kristina upped the voltage on her pleading glare. I looked away to find Duke and Quiche acting like one soul occupying two bodies.

"How much you want?" I asked, cautiously.

This was my last refuge. I wasn't paying no hundred and a half – not this time, and *not* for Frankendog. Indeed, I considered a dollar and a half nothing short of extortion.

"I don't want nothing," Zach replied. "I just want him to have a home. I can't take care of him."

You think I can?

Thankfully, I didn't say it. There were many times in former years when Kristina begged me to tell her she was adopted. That was because I embarrassed her – often on purpose. Suddenly, I realized if I hashed this deal, she might make herself an orphan.

When I opened the car door, Quiche was in like a shot. Duke was right behind. He wasn't about to allow his new friend to go anywhere without him.

Kristina was gushing with thanks and goodwill while Duke made himself at home in the co-pilot's seat. He turned toward me, his pink tongue hanging out and his brown eyes focused on me. I suspect he was laughing.

"You and me ain't gonna get along," I told him, bluntly.

He looked over his shoulder at Quiche while shedding profusely on the seat. He turned back to me and laughed again.

"Who gives a damn about you?"

Dogs don't talk. I learned that very early on. However, Duke didn't have to speak. His expression communicated volumes.

By the time we took him to the vet for a checkup and a chip, he made it clear that any friend of Quiche's was his friend as well. When he wasn't inspecting the house or being chums with Quiche, he was with me. Sometimes, he'd sit and keep watch. Sometimes, he would lay close beside my chair or my bed. Sometimes, he would sit in front of me and look at me as if I were the only person he'd ever known.

Damn and blast!

I liked him.

I liked him very much.

Unfortunately, I couldn't remember his name. I'd call him Fred or Doug or Matt or John or Dave – whatever four-letter name popped into my head. Eventually, I learned his name, but it didn't matter much. He knew I was addressing him. When he started chasing the school bus or a cyclist, however, it mattered not. I was in constant fear of a lawsuit or, worse, a crushed Duke. We agreed to keep him on a leash whenever possible. Duke, however, needs to run.

We'd take him to the disc-golf park on Saturdays. He never chased a disc. He paid no attention. However, he had to say hello to every single player. When he raced to Zack, I turned back to the car. This, I was certain, would take a while. I may as well sit down and relax.

I opened the driver's door. A brown, black and white blur shot past me and into the co-pilot's seat. He sat as demure as Shirley Temple in an old Andy Hardy film. He looked at me – again, with his tongue hanging out. He was panting, but he was also communicating.

"Where are we going now?" he seemed to ask.

Either that or "You're not getting rid of me that easy."

Where Quiche was shy and uncomfortable (except around her newest best friend), Duke was gregarious and accepting. Any time I took him around when the disc golfers were playing, Duke would greet each one individually. One school day, I had him running free in the park and a half dozen boys and girls came to play. It may have been lunch hour or a PE period at the high school just up the block. Duke sprinted over and greeted them excitedly.

He didn't know any of these young people, but they were carrying discs. That was good enough; they were friends.

Quiche has one tremendous fault. She chases deer.

One spring morning, we (foolishly) allowed Duke and Quiche to roam free around the park. They were enjoying the smells and the bracing, spring air. Then, a trio of deer wandered out of the tree line.

Game on!

Quiche was off like a shot. She doesn't bark; she runs like the wind. The deer decided this was a good time to be somewhere else. It is such simple math: the deer were faster than Quiche; Quiche is faster than Duke; Duke was faster than Kristina and me.

The deer kept just far enough ahead to tease their foolish pursuer. Duke decided it was his job to protect or, at least, be an accessory. Alas, his determination could not match the pace of the others.

It took us hours (seemingly) to get to the car. We headed in the approximate direction of the deer when last seen. Along the street, which became a rural highway beyond the residential area, we spotted Duke near a rail crossing. He recognized the car. He was ashamed. He bowed his head and looked as if he expected a beating. He'd failed to keep up with Quiche and was unable to protect her should she need protection. He didn't leap into the open door as was his wont. Instead, we had to usher him in.

We drove about town for ten minutes or so before spotting Quiche. She'd tired of the chase and was wandering aimlessly. She didn't know the way home. Her long tail was between her legs, and she knew she was lost. She perked up a bit when she saw the car, but she, too, looked as if expecting a beating.

We never beat the dogs. We swatted Quiche a couple times during her poop-in-the-house days, but that was as brutal as we ever got. Regardless, she was downcast.

By the time we returned home, the world was back on its axis, and serenity returned.

Prior to this pathetic episode, Duke didn't give a hoot about deer. If anything, he was curious. I suspect that he considered them large dogs and, therefore, potential friends. However, shy, trepidatious Quiche had pursued them with such vigor, Duke concluded it was his duty to imitate her behavior.

Two encounters cured him.

The first occurred at the park. It was not a golf day, and it was early enough that there were no other people or pets. Therefore, I let him off the leash to read his doggie newspaper at his own pace. An impudent doe sauntered out of the high grass and into view.

Game on!

I called Duke, knowing he was deaf whenever stimulated. He ignored me. Duke was determined to chase that deer to kingdom come.

Well . . . Mommy had a fawn back in the high grass. When Duke was lost from view, I rushed to the scene. He could find his way home, but I much preferred our returning together.

Just as I was near enough the grass to initiate a search, Duke came sprinting out in a wasted effort to reach Mach 1 – and the doe was hot on his tail. She took a swipe at him and, I think, she conked him on the head. A moment later, she gave up and retreated to her fawn who might need protection from some other interloper.

Duke was as contrite as an evangelist's convert. He came up to me, slowly to be sure, but he was counting on me to protect him from "that crazy woman." I could find no visible injury. If the doe did knock him on the head, he'd escaped physical damage.

A few days later, I took Duke out to a huge, vacant field where he could run, sniff, explore and be free of restraint. There was a small causeway between our neighborhood and the field. There was a doe halfway up the fence line. The sight of it was made small by the distance and neither of us gave it any thought. The next time I bothered to look, it was trotting down that fence line as if it wanted to say hello. Duke stopped where he was. He made certain of my location as he watched this crazy deer.

"I ain't afraid of you," he seemed to announce.

I swear, that deer made a complete three-hundred-sixty-degree trek around Duke. She didn't pay the slightest attention to me, but she eyed Duke with obvious malevolence. Duke was poised to defend himself if things went sour. Finally, he just sat down where he was and watched as the doe completed her patrol.

There had to be a fawn (or two) in that field somewhere. Deer, in my experience, do not display such bizarre behavior just for jollies. It may have been the same doe Duke had fled from in the disc park. Somehow, I doubt that. Regardless, the message was received – loud and clear:

"I've got my eye on you, BUSTER!"

Just as the doe was about to begin a second circuit, I called Duke.

"I think we should go home, boy."

I said it in my normal voice, devoid of histrionics. Duke, however, heard. Without the slightest hesitation, he stood up and trotted to me. For his own safety, I did not put him back on the leash until we recrossed the causeway.

After this, he and the deer get along just fine.

It isn't unusual to see deer milling about in our yard. They are quite tame (so long as there are no fawns about).

One day, Duke and I turned into the driveway with four deer lounging in the yard. I was hesitant to open my car door, but I didn't want to remain in place while waiting for the deer to move on. Once my door was open, Duke – as was his wont – jumped out.

Here we go, I thought.

He casually walked up to the front door and waited for me to open it. He paid scant attention to the deer. They, in turn, watched the scene as if we were featured entertainment.

The nearest to me, a doe, couldn't have been more than four feet away when I passed by.

We're neighbors. We get along.

Duke and Quiche will bark at the school bus, the garbage truck, joggers, and cyclists. However, they can sit by the window and watch the deer stroll by without so much as a snort.

When I take the dogs out in the morning, it is dark – particularly during the winter months. Quiche can see them, though. I can tell when she stops and stares. If I'm lucky, I might spot a pair of ears sticking up out of the darkness or the black outline of something. Duke, I'm certain, can see them as well; however, his interest is elsewhere.

When Kristina insisted that Quiche needed another dog as a live-in friend, I relented with bad grace. Duke was not a quadruped with which I cared to share the same planet. I was, practically, bullied into bringing that big, ugly brute home with us. Much to my initial disappointment, shy, retiring, quaking Quiche responded positively to Duke's proximity.

The first time we took Quiche to get a bath and pedicure, she was petrified. She didn't care for strangers, the noise, the presence of other dogs, or being handled by unfamiliar hands. She, likely, didn't care for the smells either. She didn't cry or resist, but she trembled uncontrollably the whole time. Kristina wanted to stay and calm her, but the lady (owner, manager, and sole employee) wanted us gone. The other "customers" would raise an unabated cacophony so long as there were additional people (potential rescuers) in sight.

How relieved Quiche was when we returned an hour later to take her home. She continued to tremble and dashed upstairs to hide under Kristina's bed. There she remained for quite a while.

When Duke invaded our home, we decided to get them a grooming appointment consecutively. This was Kristina's idea. She, also, insisted that Duke be first "in the gallows."

He was so friendly and trusting, he appreciated every minute of the attention he was getting. Quiche, who witnessed the entire procedure from a nearby holding pen, was calm and cooperative when it was her turn. She was happy to see us when we came for them, but she experienced no trauma.

Similarly, when an annual check-up and rabies shot (booster – whatever) was required, we took them both. When Quiche was being prodded and poked, Duke was right there. She was both malleable and cooperative. Getting a treat was welcome, of course, but the bulk of the experience was made possible by Duke's company.

These dogs never vied for either attention or treats. Kristina and I made it a standing rule that whatever one dog got, the other received the same. After morning exercise, we would cut a slice of lunch meat in half and give "lady first" and Duke next. This was SOP, and each knew the drill from the first. The only time they "argued" over food was when Kristina baked some store- bought lasagna. She put the empty baking tin down and allowed the dogs to lap up the residuals.

I scolded Kristina for that. Though no one was hurt, there were a few exciting moments before tranquility was restored. Since then, she would divide any table scraps in the respective dog bowls.

We have no set feeding time. One or the other of us will fill two bowls with the day's ration and set them on the floor near the back door. They eat when they want. When the bowls are empty (a rare occurrence), that's it. They share water bowls, one upstairs and one down, which we monitor several times a day and refill as needed.

Of course, when they go to the vet (always together), whenever the patient gets a dog treat, the "observer" gets one as well. We did not have to insist. The people at the dog hospital, both professional and volunteer, are fully aware of the share-the-spoils rule.

When my son and his family came out to visit one summer, we so wanted my grandchildren to meet the dogs. Alas, Quiche seldom gets into the car on her own. When she does, it is certain we're going either to the vet, the park, or the feed store. If she's in the car for more than five or six minutes, she gets very anxious. After "hijacking" her, twice, we agreed that she would not be subjected to a cross-state trek. Duke is a good traveler, but his reassuring presence would not sustain Quiche for hours and hours.

Brindle's former owners had a new dog both large and aggressive. They were sore afraid to have shy, little Quiche over for a visit, never mind a week-long stay. The fury motel was ruled out because Duke's calming influence was required. Our back-door neighbors had three dogs of various sizes and temperaments and were willing to take Quiche in. However, none of their dogs and Quiche had, formally, met.

We walked her over to meet the largest dog, part Dalmatian. They sniffed at each other tentatively prior to lunging. I don't know who initiated hostilities, but it was the first time I ever saw shy, petite, timorous Quiche go after another creature. When it was over, Quiche was mortified and her opponent had a split ear which bled, thankfully, only slightly.

We bought a get-well card and appended it, together with a large dog biscuit, an apology, and signed Quiche's name.

We were at our wits end. The vet would have to do, but Kristina and I shuddered to think how Quiche would suffer if left alone. She'd think we'd thrown her away. She'd simply have to come along – and hate us for the rest of her life!

The back-door neighbor came over with a plan so simple and obvious that Kristina and I were left wondering how stupid we were. The neighbor suggested if we left them a key to the house, they (the neighbors) could come in once or twice a day. They'd make certain that Quiche had food and water and they could walk her around the block twice a day.

Happy day!

Remember, we live in a small town where most people know most other people. Like the deer, neighbors are neighbors, and we help each other (particularly in winter when the snow piles up).

My son, daughter-in-law, granddaughter, and grandson would land in Portland, rent a car and join us on a whirl-wind tour. They made all the motel reservations (making certain pets were allowed).

Well, I wouldn't go to Portland to see the Second Coming. Ergo, we agreed to meet up in McMinnville and kick off our tour by going through the air and space museum.

We spent the first night with my brother and sister-in-law in Bend. We stayed in a motel with Duke. He enjoyed the dog park, just a short walk from my brother's house. He enjoyed meeting a half dozen new friends and running along behind them as they fetched tennis balls. He never did grasp the idea of chasing balls or, even, catching them. Even when someone tossed the ball right at him, he just looked at it and the person who threw it. He seemed to think they were daft.

After he collected several new friends, he went to the fence separating the big-dog area from the small-dog area. He barked as if he wanted to have the little dogs for a snack. Though his bark can rattle windows and sound vicious, Duke uses it as a salutation. He'd met all the big dogs, and he wanted to go around and make friends with the lap-dog set.

That was fun and games, but Duke required exercise at least twice a day. The dog park was fine, but he needed an opportunity to do his "business" as well. After sleeping with Kristina on her bed, he woke me at zero dark thirty, just as he did at home. I would walk him over to the field and let him run. In Bend, next to a busy highway, this was not possible. We did the best we could, but he was clearly disappointed.

We had a quick breakfast at a local fast-food joint and began our trek across the mountains. We stopped twice to look at the views. In fact, we just wanted to give Duke an opportunity to get out of the car for a few minutes. When we stopped for lunch at a favorite spot, it was hot – very hot! I left the suffering fur-shedder in the only shade in the parking lot. He couldn't go further than the length of the leash and he had only a water bowl and the asphalt for company while Kristina and I enjoyed a nice, air-conditioned meal.

I was reticent when we pulled into our hotel. Someone was bound to object. Of course, the motel accepted pets, but Duke resembled a small horse. I needn't have wasted a good worry.

Once ensconced in our *very* nice room, I took Duke for some exercise. Across the great expanse of the parking area was a vacant field separating the hostelry from the highway. There were bushes and scrub trees aplenty, and Duke explored them each in turn.

He'd been a real trooper.

When my son and his family arrived in their GPS-equipped van, the acid test awaited. I was certain Duke would like my five-year-old granddaughter and her three-year-old brother, but I had nightmarish visions of him leaping up excitedly and knocking them down.

Again, wasted angst.

Duke greeted them all as if they were long-lost friends rather than strangers. The children, in turn, treated Duke as if he was far more interesting and exciting than Grumpy Gramps.

It was blistering hot!

Minda, my daughter-in-law, checked her cell phone and found a supper emporium. I followed the GPS vehicle, and we went right to the designated spot. Alas, navigation could not aid in finding a parking space. Eventually, I had to leave poor Duke in a bake oven.

I recall only two things about our meal: it was ethnic and not much to my liking, and I was so thirsty that three fill-ups hardly dented it. Twice I left the party to check on Duke and give him a chance at some water. Again, he was super dog. He drank moderately, was grateful to be out of the car – if only for a couple minutes – and remounted the vehicle without the slightest sign of complaint.

If I'd seen a dog in a car in that heat, I'd have called the cops. I fretted about this episode for weeks, but Duke never held it against me. That was amazing.

While the my son and his wife explored the air and space museum for a good portion of the following morning, the grandkids found the play areas much more interesting. Duke and I made a detailed inspection of a nearby wood used by scouts for overnighting. It was vacant, save for Duke, me, and a few sundry joggers and cyclists who passed through.

Duke has issues with bicycles. He even came after me one morning when I went out for a spin. He bit me in the heel – well, he tried. My shoe offered sufficient protection. Nevertheless, if my newest, best friend came after me – well, his early life must have been memorable. I felt that Duke had every right to try and bite my leg off. My crime wouldn't come until much later, but it was heinous enough: no matter that I left the car windows open as much as I dared; no matter that I tended him twice and provided him water; I had subjected that dog to an hour or so in a car on, perhaps, the hottest day of the summer. Despite this despicable crime, Duke's faith and trust in me never wavered.

That makes my crime all the worse.

After the air and space museum, we hit the road for the coast. We'd stay two nights before venturing back into the furnace. It was hot on the coast, as well, but the wind provided a welcome buffer from most of it. Duke enjoyed a nice evening walk to and through a small roadside park. In the chill of early morning, we walked along the back streets of the village. He enjoyed new smells and new sights.

We took turns at the only breakfast café because someone had to watch the dog. When Kristina offered to doggie sit, I returned to watch my son and the kids chow down. The waitress recognized me from earlier. She brought me a much-appreciated coffee, *gratis.*

A whale-watching voyage was in the offing. I volunteered to stay ashore. Duke and I could have gone, the ticket-seller assured us that dogs frequently went along. I remained stubborn. If Duke got sick or (worse) had a panic attack – well, I didn't want to take the chance. He'd suffered enough in the heat the day before.

He enjoyed plying the sidewalk fronting the tourist-trap shops of the combination highway and main street of town. People, not just children, wanted to pet Duke. He enjoyed the attention.

Eventually, we settled in at a viewpoint. I sat on the bench provided; he was satisfied to sit next to me. He watched the gulls sail past and around us and strained on the leash when he discovered a chipmunk "sneaking" about. He was very patient. Perhaps, he was very satisfied to enjoy the wind, the salt air, and the view.

When the whale boat hove into view, he helped me watch it. Gradually, the swirls of color dissolved into recognizable images, I attempted to point out the kids, their parents, and Kristina. Doubtless, he thought I'd gone la-la. If he noticed either the boat or the passengers, he made no sign.

The whole contingent got sick.

Glad I didn't go. The sea didn't seem very rough, but I'd experienced a few anxious moments on previous excursions, when the sea was more placid than it was that day. Regardless, whales were sighted. The kids were plenty excited.

"Wait 'til the kids at school hear about this!"

Well, that was the sentiment I absorbed, though neither child expressed it quite that way. Neither had seen the inside of a school – yet.

Despite his size and demeanor, Duke made friends wherever we went. Curious dogs approached cautiously and found Duke most amiable and eager to make their acquaintance. Similarly, he rewarded humans with a vigorous tail wag and, occasionally, an extended paw. He warmed to children especially. During our sojourn at Crater Lake, I opted for the inviting shade of a juniper. Duke sat, pacifically, at my side and held court. He greeted anyone or anything that approached. Those who trooped past and gave a nod or a wave would get an appreciative tail wag in response.

One of Duke's primary functions, however, was to look after Quiche. He takes this task very seriously. Thrice, Quiche ran off when she had the opportunity. Duke went along as her "protector." Once, the duo returned on their own. Because Quiche is a poor navigator, I'm satisfied that Duke ushered her back to us. Other times, we had to initiate a search. When we found them, they were within a few meters of each other.

Without Duke's stabilizing influence, Quiche was in a funk. When the neighbors came by to make certain she had food and water, Quiche remained under Kristina's bed and refused to come out. They offered treats; she remained sulking and immobile. They placed treats on the stairs and pretended to leave.

No Quiche.

My backdoor neighbor, thankfully, took the liberty of propping our back door open so she could exercise and, more importantly, "do her business." Several times, he heard her running about in the back yard. Nevertheless, whenever they came into the house, Quiche went into hiding.

It was well that I didn't know this. It was doubly fortunate that Kristina had no knowledge of Quiche's behavior. Still, she remained well fed and healthy during our absence. Additionally, she got a modicum of exercise. Still, she felt betrayed.

Quiche came along with a very stout and well-made leash. In her days as Sadie, she fetched that leash whenever she desired a "walk." There were teeth marks at intervals along its length from her teething days. When we returned, we found six-to-eight-inch lengths of this leash scattered about. When she wasn't eating, drinking, doing her business, or hiding, she was chewing her leash to destruction.

She was "training" us.

Once, on Kristina's birthday, we went to the local high-end eatery for an epicurean feast. We'd left some swordfish steaks defrosting on the counter in anticipation of a second birthday dinner the following evening. Apparently, we didn't bother to properly inform Duke and Quiche of our departure. In truth, I think we snuck out of the house to avoid drama overload.

When we returned, the semi-frozen swordfish steaks were conspicuously absent. I was in a mild panic over fishbones.

"I hope you shared with Quiche," I scolded the perpetrator. "That much raw fish for one dog cannot be healthy."

Duke remained coy.

It had to be Duke. Quiche could never reach the counter, never mind grabbing them from where they lay. With experience, however, comes insight. Duke, undoubtedly, stole the fish, but it was Quiche who put him up to it.

Kristina and I, however, did not learn.

During the Christmas season, we adjourned for another expensive and celebratory feed. We made certain that we did NOT sneak away. We informed the dogs that we were leaving and assured them we would return anon.

Well, fancy dinners at a fancy diner do not sit in warming pans waiting for customers. Each meal is prepared individually. When the place is crowded, as it usually is during Yuletide, we wait, in anticipation, for our turn.

Duke and Quiche were used to our comings and goings. However, they assumed that there exists a time limit. When we failed to return after a couple hours, they decided we required remedial training.

Before our departure, Kristina made a batch of Christmas cookies she intended to decorate and distribute among our neighbors. Upon our return, there was not so much as a crumb remaining to indicate they ever existed.

"You two are going to get very sick!" she informed them.

They looked at us as if we were mentally infirm.

We didn't do nothin' their wide, innocent eyes announced.

Well, they didn't get sick. Of course, they refused to be ill, just out of spite.

Since then, we have been very careful. Whenever I make a move for the car, Duke springs into action. He *insists* on coming along, even if he isn't allowed out of the car. One day, on a whim, I leaned over into his eager expression.

"You stay, Duke," I said, softly. "You stay here with Quiche and Kristina."

He deflated. His eyes turned sad and reproachful. *But* – he turned around and went quietly back upstairs. Since that day, he will obey. All I do is say "stay." He doesn't like it, but he obeys. I can leave alone, or I can take Kristina with me. A single "stay" will suffice.

There have been no further "demonstrations" over our absence.

Duke is as handsome as Boris Karloff. Still, he attracts a lot of attention – particularly from young people. I get a glimpse from time to time. When Duke sits (awkwardly) down, he will focus his hypnotic, brown eyes on his intended "victim." He looks as prim and demure as any smaller, cuddly, "cute" dog in existence. More importantly, he is Quiche's courage.

Whenever we go to the vet, Quiche must be cajoled into the car. It's an exhausting effort at times. However, once in the car, she is as observant and curious as any dog – IF Duke in the co-pilot's seat. Perhaps, she thinks he is driving.

When we arrive, Duke dismounts instantly (usually, by bounding over me when I open the driver's door). If Duke thinks it's time to leave, there's no restraining Quiche. Once inside, she will submit to any examination, no matter the indignity, so long as Duke is nearby. Of course, when Quiche is rewarded with a treat, Duke perks up. House rules: anything one dog gets, the other gets.

Once, she had to have an x-ray. We were instructed to stay in the examination room while Quiche was "escorted" to the radiation room. Kristina and I looked at each other in wide-eyed horror. We had never heard such blood-curdling noises from any animal. Duke stood up, his curly tail at attention and his ears leaning, ominously, forward; he glared at the door. I held tightly on his leash. I sensed, from his taught body, that he was ready to rush to the rescue.

"If we have to do this again," the vet confessed upon her return, "I think we will sedate her."

If Quiche must be x-rayed again, it might be best to sedate the three of us as well.

On those rare occasions when we must be out of town for a day or three, we park the dogs at the fury motel. We want to avoid the hide-under-the-bed syndrome. Additionally, it is very likely that people, other than us, come into the house, Duke *might* consider it a hostile act. Better for our nerves and those of the insurance people that we leave the dogs with professionals. We request that they share a cell. That guarantees substantial felicity. The attendants offer copious plaudits on the well-behaved duo. With no prompting on our part, they walk Duke and Quiche together during exercise time.

When we checked them in, some months after the x-ray debacle, Quiche was fine. When we handed over the leashes, and the attendant initiated the journey down the hall to the holding cells, Quiche shook all over. She turned ragdoll and attempted to bury herself in the floor. She peed. There was no way they were getting her into the devil machine's room again!

After several anxious seconds, she happened to look up and see Duke strutting with tail wagging down the hall. Suddenly, Quiche's fears were abolished.

Wait for me! She seemed to announce.

If Duke was leading the way, fear was banished.

It's my habit to walk Duke every morning, rain or shine. I know it's time when Duke starts poking at me. Often, even in summer, it's dark when we leave the house. Weather permitting, I take Duke on a leash until we are clear of traffic and cats. Once in the huge field, I remove the leash and let him explore to his heart's content. If I'm lucky, I'll get him back on the leash. When I am not lucky, Duke patrols the neighborhood before returning to the front door. There, Quiche awaits eagerly for her turn. We three go into the back yard where Quiche chases and retrieves a rope (she doesn't like dog toys, particularly, squeaky ones) until her exercise needs are satisfied. Meanwhile, Duke mauls a bone.

One morning, I offered to take Quiche for a walk. I got the leash on her, but – *I ain't goin' out there!* I cooed at her and gently tugged a few times, but she was adamant. I don't know what magic word or gesture I used, but she, suddenly, relented. We walked out into the field. I let Duke run – knowing he would return home even if he ran off. However, I kept Quiche restricted; if she ran off, there is no telling where (or when) we'd find her.

The next morning, and every morning since, Quiche is in my room, prodding me awake. She wants to walk! If there are deer about, she spies them, even in the "inky darkness," though she never makes a fuss – no matter how close we get to them. At the conclusion of the walk, she wants to play rope.

Frequently, she wakes me at insane times. Two o'clock – three thirty – whenever she's ready. Duke, always, is right behind her. His attitude is always hopeful even when he saying *This isn't my idea.* Most times, I get up and let them outside for a bit. When I am simply unable to get up, I mumble something – anything – and they, often, flop down on the carpet and wait.

It pains me to admit that Duke was *exactly* what Quiche needed. She remains shy and timorous, but there is no situation that cannot be made acceptable so long as Duke is at hand.

I catch Duke staring at me occasionally. He looks so smug – even imperious.

I remember my initial promise about not getting along with him.

The greatest asset any dog has is the inability to talk! I am aware of my failings; I don't need some snooty dog to rub my nose in them.

Remembering Not Wisely, but Too Well

Our crew was called in from three states away. We had a pumper mounted on the bed of our vehicle, but it was bodies, not our squirt gun, that counted. We took turns driving and save for gas, snacks, and latrine visits, we drove straight through. Before we left, we loaded four cases of C-rations. The meals were well past their expiration date, but petrified food doesn't go bad. Keeping our water cans full was our top priority.

I was only three weeks out of fire camp. My companions had over a decade of experience and had worked eight or more "minor" fires and two "monsters." Our upcoming assignment was drawing on firemen from six states. I was as nervous as a cow on the opening day of deer season.

Our straw boss, Matt, was a career Forest Service man who repeatedly turned down promotions (and higher pay) because he preferred being in the forest and not behind a desk. Jack was the team smart-ass. His jokes and quips got extremely annoying, but he was the best damn worker I've ever encountered – and the bravest. Nick had two years' experience over me. He knew most of the ropes but was still learning. I didn't know a pine tree from a fir.

By the time we arrived at the base camp, it was all over but the shouting (and the overtime requests). They assigned us to search for and neutralize hot spots. It was crap duty, but it gave the regular crews a few days' much deserved rest.

It was ball-busting work, let me tell you! I took it very seriously. If we muffed our assignment, we might be responsible for letting the fire flare up and get off to the races again.

"Relax, kid," Matt advised, frequently. "If I panic, you can start worrying."

Matt was not one to panic. He knew the mission; he knew how to accomplish it.

"Keep your eye on me," he reminded. "Do what I do and remember what you learned in fire school."

After four days, we were filthy and exhausted. We smelled of smoke and pitch. Our eyes were bloodshot and stinging. There wasn't a single muscle that didn't scream or ache. When we were taken off the line, we were accorded access to a high school shower room. This was poor consolation since we had to climb into our dirty, sooty, smokey, sweaty clothes. We discussed the possibility of firing up the pumper and hosing each other down. That's how desperate we were. At the last moment, we stopped by a local bank (non-employees vacated the building with alacrity) and bought a pile of quarters. We adjourned to a local automat and coyly wrapped our nakedness in blankets or tarps.

How wonderful it felt to be in clean, non-smelly clothes again!

We wouldn't get paid until we returned home and filed piles of papers. Until then, we had only what we brought with us. Fortunately, there are few opportunities to purchase anything in what remained of a once forested area. Pooling our cash, we had a few pennies above forty dollars. The government credit card was only for gas. Therefore, we faced three or four days on the road with forty dollars.

All eyes focused on Matt.

"We still have a few dollars in quarters," he reminded.

It was his way of telling us that there were plenty of C-rations left over.

By now, we concluded that eating the tin cans was more appealing than gagging on their contents.

"Keep your eye on me," Matt suggested.

This anodyne had served us well during our "mop up" operation; there was little reason to discard it.

Forty-eight miles down the road, we entered a speed zone. In that poor excuse for habitation, there was a highway department maintenance shed keeping company with three small mountains of crushed rock. There was a post office in a brick building so small, we could have loaded it on the bed of our rig if we were insane and determined. There was, also, a small hash house set up in what was once a one-room schoolhouse. The residents of this tiny burg were scattered hither and yon on an expansive alluvial plane. We could see a half dozen homesteads within sight of the highway. Undoubtedly, there were many more we could not see.

All eyes were on Matt. He felt the heat. He slowed down and turned into the café's "parking lot," a small patch of compacted dirt. There wasn't much parking area left after our rig came to a stop.

We entered, single file, to discover a counter with three stools, a booth with green plastic upholstery repaired with frequent applications of duct tape. There was a table with two folding chairs to handle any "overflow." Behind the counter was a partition with a second counter, high up and wide enough for us to see cooking utensils on shelves or hanging from knobs and hooks.

Once crammed into the booth, a woman in a white dress, apron and shoes sallied forth.

She was big! She did her best to fill the "dining area." She produced two hand-printed menus and set them down so nobody would be forced to read upside down. At this point, she glared. It was obvious from her expression that she considered us no better than a truck load of cow pats. In particular, she eyed Nick with distain.

Nick is a soft-spoken young man who could work his ass off for twelve consecutive hours on any task assigned. He took care of all the forms and cards with which our crew must contend. His was only a high school education, but he spoke and understood *bureaucrat* so fluently that he often had our superiors in a quandary. When it came to chopping, lifting, grubbing, planting, or most any manual labor, he could do the work of we three working in concert.

Nick was Japanese American, and proud of it. His parents met in one of the "camps" during the war. They, too, were American. Nevertheless, Nick made a close study of both his cultures. He spoke Japanese. He spoke *Merican*, both the slangy version we used on the job and the brand best suited for the erudite.

He was proud of his dual heritage. He never appeared in public without his amulet. It was a small but detailed lapel pin with crossed American and Japanese flags. It was the meatball that stoked the waitress/cook/proprietor's boiler.

"I don't serve Japs," she announced in a tone decidedly uncivil.

We all sat in stunned silence for a moment. Matt, eventually, cleared his throat.

"Nick, will you wait for us in the rig?"

Jack and I looked at Matt with bottomless incredulity. Nick was a team member. We were one for all and all for one! How could Matt be so brutal? This was not right.

"Remember Pearl Harbor!"

This battle cry issued from the mouth of the red-faced woman. There was considerable hate behind it.

"Do as you're told," was the adjunct to "Keep your eye on me." None of us would debate an issue with Matt. His word was law – and he had the muscle to back it up.

When he issued an order, none of us dared to initiate discussion. However, Jack and I sent a look Matt's way which could not be mistaken for amiability.

We watched as Nick shuffled out the door.

"I'll have the pork chops," Matt boomed. "Extra applesauce."

Keep your eye on me.

Jack and I followed suit.

The woman nodded, cast a glance through the window to make certain Nick was making no effort to return.

"My brother was on the *West Virginia*," she explained to us. "It took them three days to find his body."

Matt nodded.

"I understand," Matt replied.

I was about to author some caustic remark about banishing Nick, but I held my tongue. Jack was senior to me. It was his place, not mine. I was miffed at him for not speaking up.

Matt brought his map in with him. After a prolonged and silent study, he slid it across the table and turned it round for Jack's edification. He poked a small square near a road junction. Jack focused. After a few moments of study, he slid the map back from whence it came.

"That's pushing past a hundred and fifty miles," Jack advised.

"Hurry up, Grandma!" Matt bellowed. "We're damned hungry out here."

"Extra applesauce!" Jack reminded.

"Don't get a hard on! Unless ya like yer pork chops raw, yer gonna have to wait."

We couldn't help but hear. However, we three ignored her bellowing.

"There's three eating places," Matt reminded. "And two supermarkets."

I did not understand the purpose of this exchange.

"We ain't gonna make it home today," Jack calculated. "Even if we drive all night, we can't make it."

"And we can't afford a motel room," Matt nodded. "We can go up one of these fire roads a mile or so and sleep out. I ain't drivin' all night again."

We'd taken turns to get to the fire and on the line as soon as possible. It was miserable. There was no way we could get any sleep worthy of the name. The only rest we accrued was when one of us dozed off at the wheel for a few seconds. Luckily, there was at least one restless passenger to raise the alarm. None of us wanted to stretch our luck any further.

Jack looked at me. I looked back. We had wasted precious space by tossing our sleeping bags onto the bed of the truck, but we never got to use them. With the temperature what it was, we'd not use them on our return, unless one of us had ambitions of death by broiling.

"Let's not make camp before we've had some eats," Jack suggested.

Matt folded the map, unbuttoned his shirt, and stowed the map between his outer garment and his sweat-laden t-shirt.

Realizing, yet again, that I had no idea what this conversation was about, I opted to remain silent. That, however, did not inhibit the whirl of question marks inside my head.

We sat in silence.

"Granny," Matt yelled, "we could raise our own hogs in the time it's takin' you!"

We heard a snort emanating from near the grill.

Finally, here came three plates attached to the stout woman's upper appendages.

"Here she comes," Jack, who was facing the kitchen, whispered.

Matt slid out of the booth.

"Sorry, grandma. We gotta shove off."

The woman froze in wide-eyed disbelief as Jack rose, followed by me.

"You bastards!" she bellowed, her face turning cherry red.

We shuffled to the door.

"Remember Hiroshima, Granny!" Matt shouted over his shoulder as he exited.

"You sorry sons-a-bitches!" She screamed.

Nick, by virtue of his banishment, had first pick of the remaining Cs. He was eating pork and beans out of a can.

"Ham and eggs," Matt announced, putting his bid in early.

Ham and eggs is the least unpalatable selection.

Jack made a grab for spaghetti and meatballs. I didn't bother to look; I just grabbed.

Beefsteak!

I opened the package, rolled down my window and tossed the can out. I'm not a litterbug by habit. However, there was room for me in the van or room for the beefsteak, but not both of us. In the human food department, C-ration beefsteak comes just above radioactive mud.

The canned bread was almost as bad as the beefsteak, but I needed something in my stomach, no matter how deplorable. In fire school, an instructor explained how a person can make a pudding out of C-ration canned bread.

I opened the can with my ever-ready P-38. I chopped it up with my not-so-clean pocketknife and added sugar and dry creamer. To this, I added water from our cabin thermos and stirred. I added a "pinch" of instant coffee and stirred some more. I saved the candy patty for dessert.

This was far from satisfying, but it kept my stomach from adding to my misery.

After thirty minutes, Matt pulled over and changed places with Jack. He could eat while driving, but Matt took safety very seriously. Moreover, Jack was just as good a driver as Matt, particularly on a mostly deserted highway.

The remains of our repast (save for my beefsteak) were stowed in a designated trash bag.

"What gives, Matt?" Jack asked after a very quiet spell.

Matt sighed before answering.

"I didn't handle that situation very well. Sorry guys."

"The bitch had it coming," Jack assured.

Matt remained mute for some while, but he was thinking hard. He's good at it. His thinking saved us considerable time and wasted effort on our brush-disposal patrols. Keeping the fire roads open was the most important part of our non-firefighting job. Indeed, it was the reason for our summer employment.

"It's been thirty-three years," Matt stated at last. "It takes a heap of energy to carry that much hate around."

"Come on, boss. Nick had nothing to do with Pearl Harbor."

"I was still a gleam in my pappy's eyes," Nick confirmed.

That sentence was, purposely, as non-Japanese as he could make it. Yes, he was Japanese, and proud of it. However, he was an American. He mightn't look it but talking and sounding like Chester Proudfoot underscored his feelings.

"Your folks hold a grudge, Nick?"

I recognized my voice. As the low man on an otherwise experienced crew, I made it a practice to hold my tongue. On this occasion, nobody objected.

"Of course, they do," Nick replied. "It ain't nothin' like that woman back there, though."

"I heard the camps were real hell holes," Jack injected.

"For the troublemakers, for certain. Mom an' Pop was in a less hostile environment. It was cramped as hell and food was rationed – just like on the outside, but there were no beatings or executions. They turned it into a decent little town – a church, a school, small businesses, you know – seamstresses and tool makers. They ran a slate of candidates and elected a mayor, a town council and even a sheriff. During good weather, they could leave the camp and plant crops – well, during the day, anyway."

"Sounds like what we went to war to protect," Matt said. "Doesn't sound so bad."

"Well, it wasn't. Remember, though, they were forced to live there; all the property they left behind was confiscated."

"Yeah, and you didn't have to get into the fight."

"There were many people willing to go," Nick reported. "I think, some did, but I don't know there of any from the camp my folks was in."

There was a considerable pause.

"You wanna drive again, boss?"

"You're doing just fine. When you get tired, just pull over, and I'll take it."

He resumed brooding.

"I wonder how my family would react if I got called up and killed?" He asked at last.

Three of the crew were sitting comfortably on their draft deferments. Matt had a bum leg; Jack was colorblind; and Nick had some endocrinology snafu. I had a higher number, but that was no guarantee I'd slide.

"You think they will spend the rest of their days hating Asians?"

"God! I hope not."

"If someone is shooting at me," Nick concluded. "I'll shoot back. Otherwise, I'll leave the bastard alone."

"My folks would likely hate the people who sent me," Jack mused aloud.

Matt sighed.

"I could have handled that better," he repeated.

"Want me to turn around?" Jack asked. "You could – I don' know – apologize?"

"What would we tell the boss when he goes over the gas receipts?"

This required no answer. Our Fire Control Officer was the one Federal employee who was conscientious about government spending. He is not noted for his understanding nature.

The World Turned Upside Down

Paisley studied herself in the full-length mirror provided by the not-so-plush hostelry. The image she examined was neatly arrayed. Her ankle-length culottes (split skirts, her preferred diction) and her matching vest were tailor-made. There was not a spot or wrinkle to be detected. The white blouse peeked out timorously from the miniscule vest aperture. The broad, white collar was a mistake – it lapped over the back and shoulders of the vest like an odious bed sheet.

I should have been more careful about the blouse, she mused. Well, it was too late to make amends. The car would come soon.

She inspected her shoes, brand new but, also, made to order. They were comfortable. They added three inches to her height, but Paisley balked at any of the more "trendy" heels. She was celebrating a reunion – not auditioning for the cover of *Vogue*.

She eschewed jewelry. Paisley wanted to look "nice" while attracting as little attention as possible.

In a surge of vanity, she was about to model for the mirror, but checked herself in time. Facing her image, full frontal, she enjoyed the attractive view of her new togs. To examine herself in profile or from behind – well, she was "without form and void."

Paisley was the name of the son and heir. When her father, Lord Harcourt, discovered the gender of his firstborn he was not pleased. The fact that his daughter resembled a boy through puberty did nothing to curb his disappointment. Paisley and Wilfred, her brother, were very close. They shared the same tutors and the same passion for cricket. Because of the three years separating them, Paisley held a decided advantage for most of their lives at home.

There was one rite of passage that traumatized Paisley both before and during: eating at table. Until a child reached its thirteenth year, it was fed earlier and separately. For three weeks, leading up to her birthday, Paisley was schooled in proper table etiquette. It was bad enough to have Wilfred looking on and snickering, but she trembled when the evening came for her to dine with mater and pater. It was seldom that the trio dined together, one or the other of her parents was often away "on business." Papa scolded when Paisley's decorum lapsed. Mama, habitually, cleared her throat to signal violations of proper behavior. It was preferable to dine with Mama. "State dinners," when all three plus a guest (or a half-dozen) were present, Paisley ate both carefully and sparingly.

"You must eat more!" Lord Harcourt insisted.

"With my stomach knotted and my nerves frayed? How?"

She thought this repeatedly, but never uttered it.

Paisley much preferred eating with Wilfred. Save for surreptitious "snacks," such opportunities were denied after that dreaded, unlucky thirteen!

Praise God!

On those days when father and mother were both away, the children ate in the kitchen with the servants. Oh, these were such jolly times!

Paisley went through tutors like a surgeon goes through gauze. Harcourt was impressed, but much of his attention was devoted to Wilfred. Lady Harcourt, however, encouraged her daughter in all things. Paisley would peer over her mother's shoulder when composing her weekly newspaper column. Tentatively, at first, she would suggest specific edits.

"It sounds better," Paisley would insist after reading the original and her suggested replacement back-to-back.

She was brilliant enough to employ snappy syntax but too unschooled to explain why. Lady Harcourt seldom hesitated to enlighten her daughter. Within weeks, Paisley became a walking lexicon. She sang snippets of favorite opera libretto. Unfortunately for her family, Paisley's expertise in composition and rhetoric far outstripped her vocal talent. When encouraged by anyone within earshot to retreat beyond earshot, the girl "took the hint" and kept her voice to herself. However, her pen scratched out poetry with alarming dexterity. After reading Pope's translation of the *Iliad,* she produced scores of pages in rhymed couplets. Her most judicious work was a "translation" of *Alice Through the Looking Glass* into Pope's meter and couplets.

Lady Harcourt used her influence (and no little of her husband's) to deliver Paisley into the hands of those better suited to her temperament and her insatiable appetite for language.

It took considerable pressure, but Paisley was accepted into college at the age of fourteen. She couldn't reside at college due to liability issues; therefore, she and an employed "companion" took private lodgings in town. Paisley was escorted, daily, to and from college for two years.

Her "fellows" (it was a women's college) accepted her early on. She not only impressed them with her literary prowess, but they called upon her capacious knowledge of letters and literature to help them with their own studies. She looked like a young "girl," but she could converse with anyone – from the provost and dons to the scouts – and in their own language. Further, she knew, instinctively, when the high Oxford diction was called for, but preferred the more casual, less-snooty locution of her fellow students.

One of the first to "fall under her spell" was Doris Grew, another first-year "fellow," four years older who reverted to her Yorkshire dialect when not "on parade." Doris was "middle class," but endeared herself to Paisley by dismissing the awkward aristocratic pedigree. In return, Paisley never looked down on Grew's "common" lineage. Their genuine affection for each other transcended both their age and class differences. Doris treated Paisley as an equal; Paisley reciprocated.

One of Paisley's first tasks was to research and report on the "economic and social ramifications resulting from the ascension of James I." Doris helped with the early research by introducing the precocious child to the college librarian and the special collections left in her charge. Periodically, she checked up on her young protegee's progress. Researching and correctly recording her findings was – um – "child's play" for the youngest member of her class. Composing an acceptable essay, however, was a study in frustration. No matter how Paisley formatted her research findings, her efforts struck her either as frustratingly pompous or amateurish (even "childlike"). After three abortive attempts and with only hours prior to a scheduled meeting with her tutor, the girl tore up her drafts and began anew.

She was the topic of conversation in the senior common room for days. The tutor was impressed by Paisley's interpretations and conclusions, but a scholarly paper submitted in Spenserian quatrains did not promote felicity. This simply wasn't done! Was this young girl thrusting her nose in the air or was she in earnest?

A few of the dons wanted her tossed – such a young girl, no matter how precocious, had no business in an academic institution; she should be sent home until she gained some semblance of maturity. Eventually, the warden was called upon to quell what was fast becoming a rebellion.

"Did she research thoroughly and correctly?" she asked Paisley's tutor.

"Quite so."

"Did she present and defend her conclusions?"

"With one or two exceptions, she did. I dare say, she did better than most first-year students – in my experience."

The warden read the text the previous evening, but she paged through the material once more.

"First, Miss Sanderson, I expect you to lecture Miss Newland-Atwood on the proper means of submitting research papers. She's not yet fifteen. I think we can afford her some latitude. Also, emphasize that – until her linguistic skills are up to snuff – she must refrain from inserting these Latin phrases and passages. They hurt my head just looking at them."

There was a hush. The "speech from the throne" left no room for further protestations. At high table that night, the warden injected an addendum.

"As Miss Newland-Atwood has demonstrated her proclivity for verse, it might be in her best interest – and ours – if we gently nudge her into letters and languages."

She addressed no one. It was merely the scholarly head of the college thinking out loud. However, the nudging commenced and not without result. Beginning immediately, Paisley refrained from using Latin asides unless quoting Roman authors or medieval scholars.

The first few months, Paisley was escorted to the college by her female companion. Thereafter, Doris would wake early and fetch her to morning chapel. When the scholastic day was finished, she escorted her back to lodgings. It was a task she enjoyed mightily. They talked about a myriad of topics. It was during these peripatetic colloquies that Paisley was introduced to the concept and practice of sex. Lady Harcourt had provided "certain fundamentals" prior to Paisley's leaving home, but Doris was not nearly as "careful" in tone or content as was mater.

As with her scholastic efforts, Paisley absorbed her "sex lectures" as a sponge laps up water. In truth, the idea of sex frightened her. She was slow to make male friends – and was very wary. These qualities served her well when she met *the* man she fancied. It didn't last long – she was still underage – but *damn*; it was fun!

Doris helped Paisley become "normal." Her life B.D. (before Doris) was filled with people who fawned over the "genius" child and praised her and used her as a living parlor trick. Paisley allowed people's admiration and praise to go to her head. Even at college, third years deferred to her despite being jealous or envious of her mental acuity. Doris, however, treated her as a friend and confidant. True, she called upon Paisley to help her with math and chemistry – she'd have been a fool to not to. The girl, eager to be of service, explained and simplified concepts and problem solving; she taught Doris *how* to do rather than doing the work for her. In return, Doris was an ace at language skills and helped Paisley improve her Latin. What she learned from Doris served her well later when Paisley took up the study of ancient Greek.

The two were inseparable. A few of the dons feared that they might be "too close." When Paisley began her third year, it was decided that she could (and should) live at the college with the other undergraduates. There was a brief scene when Doris remained in the East Hall while Paisley was dispatched to the Old Wing. The two were separated by half the college.

Not until she was a resident did Paisley enter the junior common room for the first time. Previously, she would work in the library or an empty lecture room. She feared the older students and preferred to keep her distance. However, the JCR was the logical place to meet up with Doris before chapel and during the day.

Paisley was nervous when she left the library on Saturday morning. Doris had a dentist appointment and promised to meet her in the JCR after lunch.

There were eight "fellows" in the common when Paisley entered. Five were on the far end of the lounge, smoking cigarettes and chatting away frivolously, though one third year held an open text on her lap. Two more sat together on a sofa chatting with their robes carelessly heaped in the remaining space. The remaining girl sipped tea from a mug while paging through a magazine. To Paisley's relief, no one paid her the slightest attention.

The JCR was divided equally between the smokers and non-smokers. There was nothing so crude as a border fence or a painted white line, but the ash trays were conspicuously confined to a particular area. The "Jacobite section" (a tongue-in-cheek moniker in honor of the anti-smoking monarch) was reserved for those who did not enjoy the smell of cigarette smoke or residual aromas clinging to clothes.

Paisley's heart was racing. Despite her erudition, she remained a child among mature – or very nearly mature – women. She clutched her volume of *Tristram Shandy* (a gag gift from Doris) and padded softly to the nearest Jacobite armchair. The girl with the tea and magazine paused, momentarily, to investigate. She smiled hello and returned to her reading.

Paisley recognized her as a second-year student who resided in East Hall. The "child" was ignorant of this person's name, but she, obviously, knew Paisley – and, likely, by name. She made no fuss, hurled no pejorative, nor had she treated her as a freakish celebrity; she did nothing beyond sending a much appreciated if tacit message of collegiality. Paisley had as perfect a right to be in the JCR.

What a relief!

Doris Northcutt (*Grew* as was) examined herself in the mirror. She was both excited and trepidatious about seeing Paisley again. She wore a stylish suit which helped moderate the eight pounds she'd acquired since going down. She'd delivered two children and had suffered a certain sedentary existence for far too long. She'd been most active for the previous eight months and succeeded in shedding five pounds, but –

Doris wondered if Paisley had "bulked up" during their years apart. Unlike Doris, however, her young friend could use a few extra pounds. The images she'd seen confirmed that Paisley Newland-Atwood, still unwed, was as beautiful as ever. However, the pictures in journals and newspapers were confined to the young woman's visage. When they'd parted ways, Paisley had no bust and no butt – well not enough of either to create a noticeable silhouette. Nevertheless, behind that beautiful face, perfect smile, and flashing eyes resided a capacious and highly efficient brain. Additionally, Paisley could read the ingredient list from a box of crisps and recite it as perfectly enunciated and resonant as an experienced Shakespearian actress.

That was the ticket!

Doris went down with a first in Ancient History. Paisley went down with a first in Letters. Doris had established herself as a top-flight researcher; her tomes of Bronze Age Greece and Roman Africa were highly lauded amongst scholars.

Her monograph on Greece became required reading in several universities in Britain, France, and Germany. Paisley confined her efforts to scholarly journals and were limited in length. They were, however, highly praised and portions were often quoted in intellectual circles.

The Beeb wanted to do a series. Three hour-long episodes on Roman Britain. Doris put in a bid. She envisioned an examination of the auxiliary troops.

"The legions have been beaten to death," she insisted.

The BBC was hoping she'd drag in that mysterious Ninth Legion, the one that "disappeared" on the soggy isle. There were theories galore about what happened to it, but, as Doris emphatically pointed out, without serious archeological evidence, the theories – signally or combined – were little more than an academic striptease.

"Why the auxiliaries?" some bold official asked.

"Because they came here from all over the empire," Doris reminded. "They came as homogeneous groups, not like the legions that accepted recruits from hither and yon. We can travel to Romania, Algeria, Germany, Spain. We can trace the existing towns and villages where these people came from. We even know some of their names. No few retired here. Some deserted and started a new life. Some were captured and made slaves. They married native women. They raised families. They are our ancestors as much as the Saxons and Normans."

That piqued interest.

When the BBC formally contacted her, Doris thought of Paisley. If Doris could gather the materials, Paisley could punch out the scripts. Further, Paisley could be the presenter. Doris got clammy and wobbly whenever she presented a lecture, and her voice was nowhere as polished as Paisley's. The big-wigs at the Beeb would drool over Paisley's voice and spot-on enunciation. It wouldn't hurt to advertise that Paisley would inherit a title. Further, if she did the writing *and* the presenting, the company could save a bundle in expenses. True, the BBC had a reputation for spending a million quid to teach hippos to dance (this hyperbolic charge was leveled during a chat show – a BBC chat show). Now, however, the crunch was on; spending was not so free as in "the old days."

The idea that evolved into the history of Roman auxiliaries in Britain was sparked by Paisley. *Through* Paisley might be more accurate.

Doris and Paisley were committed to gaining their M.A. They planned a celebratory break before "hitting the books again," as Doris described it. They reserved a tour of Greece. This would broaden Doris's historical horizon while Paisley, a neophyte in ancient Greek, would have the opportunity to examine ancient engravings while attempting to make herself understood by modern Greeks. As with all flights of fancy, it was sure to be more enjoyable than didactic. They would, also, suffer acute embarrassment several times a day, but they were as giddy as any first-year student.

Amid the ruins of Tiryns, the excited duo followed a guide through an impressive and intact sally port. Through this aperture, the guide informed, the sentries would report to their assigned posts and return. Over many decades, the leather shoulder "armor" not only eroded a noticeable crease in the rock, they polished the stones.

"My God, Paise!" Doris gasped. "You're taller than these fierce, hulking soldiers of the *Iliad*."

Paisley turned to inspect her vivacious companion. Doris pointed to her discovery. There was no denying that the precocious girl's shoulder, *sans* Bronze-age armor, was noticeably above the grove formed by veritable legions of garrison soldiers. For "Paise," it was an interesting observation but unworthy of further cogitation. For Doris, it was the key that opened a Bronze-age treasure trove.

The heroes of Troy and Thermopylae were pip-squeaks compared with twentieth-century males! It was a realization that burrowed into her consciousness. When her studies led her through the Roman conquest, she reminded herself that Caesar's legionaries were hardly much larger and bulkier than Agamemnon's troops. Were the Germans similarly dwarfish? That didn't seem possible. How about the tribes of Britain? Whenever she researched an ancient culture, she began by studying the skeletal remains of the males. Some of the auxiliary troops assigned to Britain may have been of greater stature. Maximinus Thrax, the huge and imposing emperor, came from "barbarian" stock.

Perhaps – just perhaps – warrior size might, partially, account for part of the "restlessness" in the Roman provinces.

Save for a brief visit to the museum archive years before, Paisley was a stranger to Norwich. She hired a car and driver. It was her means of ensuring that "nothing went awry" rather than a show of ostentation. She felt a fraud (or a fool) when her hireling held the rear door open for her and made certain of her comfort before sealing her in. Paisley prayed that Doris and she would not arrive at their agreed upon venue simultaneously; that would send an unintended message.

When the vehicle pulled up into an "unloading zone," Paisley fought the urge to fling herself out of the car to reduce the chances of Doris witnessing the event. However, she refused to flaunt custom. She bit her lip and waited (for ages) as her driver came around and opened her door. The woman was as precise in exiting as she'd been when entering; she would not risk damaging or wrinkling her livery.

"Thank you, sir," she said while scolding herself for not properly introducing herself to her coachman.

She vowed to put matters right during her return journey. She did not want to appear haughty any more than she desired to appear snooty.

"Please, call for me in two hours."

The young man – and he was decidedly young – replied with a silent nod. She'd worn that distinction of "decidedly young" herself during her undergraduate days – and for some time after. She'd avoid judging others.

She looked furtively about while doing her best not to appear furtive. There was no sign of Doris.

Good!

She entered the hostelry unaided, making the staff wary and suspicious. Even in the post-feminist era, unescorted woman in posh venues set off silent alarms.

"I'm meeting a colleague," she announced, trying hard to sound casual. "Mrs. Northcutt has reserved a table, I believe."

Paisley was dissatisfied with both her announcement and her demeanor. She'd been long enough in America to be at home with the relaxed and informal atmosphere. Back on British soil, social etiquette was in a continual state of flux. Being too traditional was as likely to spoil the atmosphere just as completely as being too "modern."

The captain appeared satisfied, but, of course, appearances didn't count for as much as they once had.

"Mrs. Northcutt awaits," he responded with a smile.

No *Miss* or *Madam*? Perhaps, Paisley wasn't the only person intent on avoiding an unintended *faux pas*. His erect posture and confident, long strides were impressive. Not for the first time did Paisley consider the upscale eatery a mistake. A local fish and chips would have served as well – even better when one considered the fuss and bother of fine duds and time spent primping. However, Mrs. Northcutt, M.A. and Paisley Harcourt, M.A. were well along on their course for doctorates in their respective fields. Too informal a setting mightn't serve.

When Paisley "hove into view" behind the prim captain, Doris shot up out of her chair as if she'd been perched on a giant spring. The two *ladies* greeted each other with a mighty hug.

They were undergraduates again!

When the hugs and greetings were exhausted, they were assisted into their respective seats.

"Would the ladies desire a cocktail before dinner?"

There it was – that stiff, toothachingly correct manner and diction.

Doris and Paisley eyed each other mischievously for only a moment.

"I'd like a sidecar," Doris announced.

"A horse's neck for me, please," Paisley added.

The captain did not bow, but he acknowledged their desires with a prim, non-verbal gesture.

Doris and Paisley smiled. They may well have sent the barman in search of a book of long-forgotten lore. Does anybody still order such antiques?

Once the captain was beyond earshot, the two women burst into a subdued peel of undergraduate giggles.

Visitors

My retirement house is excellently situated. Save for my back-door neighbors, all the homes in and near our development are much of a football field (or more) distant. There is a considerable amount of land undeveloped. Duke and Quiche, our canine co-residents, have ample area to explore without leaving "souvenirs" to provoke the local populous. Since our abode is nestled in the high desert, we are frequently visited by no few of the natives. Hawks, quail, and a variety of feathered "friends" abound. I have seen bald eagles at close range. Geese and ducks migrate with the seasons in incredible numbers.

There are a few malevolent creatures in and around our village. Cougars have been killed within the urban boundary though, thankfully, not often. I frequently hear coyotes howling in the early morning. A friend relates how the largest rattlesnake he'd ever seen was sunning itself near the public pool. Normally, he'd have let it be, but it was too close to children, and he dispatched it. For a time, wolves (imported by government agencies) terrorized nearby farms and ranches. We, also, have a musk ox, also imported, which has become a local tourist attraction.

My daughter's dog, Quiche, discovered a litter of skunks in a nearby field. The babies were curious and friendly. They and Quiche were instant friends. Fortunately, mama was off (foraging, I suppose) or the encounter might have proved disastrous.

Quiche, also, attempted to make friends with a garter snake. The reptile didn't want anything to do with our curious dog and found refuge in some tall, thick grass.

I find evidence of badgers in the largest of the nearby fields, but – to date – I've yet to see one. That is one record, I sincerely hope, is never broken.

There is one quadruped that is ubiquitous in our small environ: the deer. Many have become "townies," that is, they live here all year round. During hunting season, those less domesticated creatures unerringly find their way into town; they, apparently, know they cannot be hunted here. The "visitors," or "refugees" if one prefers, are readily identified. They are skittish and unsettled; they will race for cover when approached or whenever subjected to loud noises.

The town is split nearly fifty-fifty when it comes to deer. Half consider them pests, disease carriers, and tick transporters. Further, any arborist hates them since gardens and flower beds constitute the deer equivalent of confectionary shops. One person reported that roses are, for a deer, ice-cream sundaes. Those few who have lush gardens or floral displays either stand twenty-four-hour watches or own a large, loud dog.

I have seen deer cross a field, diagonally, at a slow lope – all twenty-seven of them! Normally, they roam the streets in trios, quintets, and sextets. Of course, no few are killed or injured by residents who drive too fast, while inebriated, or both. I, myself, had to call the game warden to remove a dead deer from our street.

Deer are pretty smart, despite all propaganda to the contrary. They use the crosswalks in town and keep to the side of the street in the residential areas. They know the location of every apple tree and keep the surrounding area devoid of windfalls. They know the difference between friendly dogs and hostile ones. A loud dog will not intimidate a townie; it must be loud *and* aggressive. The deer know exactly where such dogs live and, wisely and unerringly, eschew them.

The deer's Achilles heel, however, is keeping itself and its family safe and healthy. The bucks seldom hang around with the does except during mating season. The fawns and yearlings keep near mama during the winter months. Mama will bed down her fawn (often two) and graze alone during the morning. She, generally, rousts the young ones out in the afternoon and they feed together. The fawns will remain quiet and still when left alone. If anyone or anything gets too near them, a doe can be deadly. No few dogs are trampled, and some are killed, by a doe protecting her young.

When food is scarce, or after a heavy snow, the deer will resort to extreme measures. I've seen deer on their hind legs nibbling at tree leaves they normally ignore. They are opportunists. They work hard to keep their stomachs full in case they are forced, by circumstances, to go without food for a few days.

Our neighbors keep a nice little flower garden near their driveway. They spend a lot of time planting and spaying and trimming and babying their delightful display. One afternoon, I stopped and asked how they kept the deer from chowing down on their plants.

"I just plant things deer don't eat," came the reply.

What a simple solution! I wondered why other gardeners hadn't thought of this.

After a particularly malevolent spell of weather, however, I looked out my kitchen window one morning and found a small group of deer making quick work of the neighbor's pride and joy.

A few days later, the neighbor woman stopped for a coffee in the local chat-and-chew. I'd never seen her in the establishment before. Likely, her regular take-away was out of service due to weather conditions. I said hello but couldn't resist reporting that I'd noticed she'd had visitors recently.

She was furious, but not at me. I won't record what she said – much of it was of Anglo-Saxon origins. Suffice it to say that deer, when forced, will eat items they'd never touch otherwise.

Recently, there was a newspaper story, complete with a photo, of a doe who limped, slowly, behind the hospital. She lay down, just behind the maternity ward, and dropped her fawns. Both patients and staff witnessed the performance from the windows. Being gawked at by humans behind glass bothered neither mama nor her newborns. Deer are wary of people, but anyone approaching slowly seldom bother or frighten them.

My church is located on the highway north of town and adjacent to a cow pasture. Owing to our tiny congregation, we meet downstairs in the event room and kitchen area; it's cooler in the summer and easier to heat in the winter. One day, three deer wandered about, lowered their heads to peer at us through the windows, and were mesmerized by our gathering. When the sermon commenced, they lay on their stomachs and attended closely. The moment the sermon terminated (I swear this is true), all three got up, as if on command, and wandered off.

Because of this, and several other episodes, I have come to feel that the deer are our neighbors, every bit as much as those who live near and service us: the sanitation people, delivery personnel, street crews, mail lady, and others who keep our end of town up and running. We recognize the "lone ranger," a doe that was orphaned a few years ago. She's grown now and, generally, tags along after other groups. None of them will accept her, for reasons unclear to humans. They don't mind her following, but they make clear they do not desire her company.

Another doe dropped her fawns in a nearby field. For this trio, my daughter and I have taken a proprietary interest. This, in no small part, was engendered by Mommy's tolerance of us. She was used to seeing the dogs and me walking in the huge, empty field on our side of town. After she delivered her fawns, she would lay with them and calmly watch our morning routine. Duke, who had learned not to bother deer mothers, runs free in search of new smells. Occasionally, he will bully a pair or an entire flock of geese into flight, but he will not approach the doe – especially when her fawns are near. Quiche, we keep on a leash. She's very curious about the deer family and will launch like an arrow after them if we turn her loose. Momma deer knows this and keeps us under close observation. However, we can pass within a few feet of each other without any show of hostility or fear on either side.

This family comes to and through our yard frequently. We started a routine of slicing up apples and leaving them along the edge of our driveway. She and her fawns appreciate our offering. Other groups began gathering up our apple slices. It is first-come-first-served.

My daughter and I try to keep a supply of apples or baby carrots handy. Since some of our two-legged neighbors don't care to have a congregation of deer about, we try to be subtle. In the dark of the morning – particularly during the winter months when forage gets scarce – I will slice up an apple or two and lay them out along the edges of our driveway. When these disappear, we know that one or more "visitors" have come by. Occasionally, we will see them raiding us. Eventually, my daughter decided that she'd like to hand-feed our mule-eared friends.

This was a project.

First, our visitors had to accept our appearance without bolting for the safety of distance. This was accomplished early on. We would feed them by tossing bits of apples of carrots in the vicinity of a particular deer. Naturally, we concentrated on the younger deer. There exists, however, a pecking order. The larger deer will nudge or chase a fawn or yearling away and intercept our offering. Whenever we attempted to approach, they would quickly move away to maintain a safety zone between us.

Next, we would hold out an offering. A few would come near, but they remained very wary. They would not accept food unless (or until) we dropped it and stepped back. Eventually, if one of us came outside the house, the "regulars" recognized us. They associated our presence with food and would approach. In time, their "approach" morphed into a "come-and-get-it."

I managed to hand feed a couple deer which disappointed my daughter. She likes to sleep late and misses out. My success irked her enough to bring her down one morning when we were fresh out of apples and carrots. We had a few grapes, however, which the deer find delightful. My daughter was positively giddy when an impatient deer snatched a grape from her fingers while her attention was elsewhere.

After three or four years of feeding, we know the "regulars" from the "guests." The former will come right up to us – particularly the doe with the twin fawns and their "friend," a doe with a gnarled eye and no fawns. These friends seldom hesitate to approach. The "guests" will stand back and insist we toss them snacks. This is frustrating because the target we select, inevitably gets shunted aside by one of the bullies. Strangely, the boldest of our guests are, also, the youngest. Apparently, they have not completed their training and will come right up to us. Not all of them are so inclined. Many youngsters keep distance. Only a select few throw caution to the winds.

One morning, we entertained an entire gang. There were, at least, eight of various ages. My daughter took a handful of grub and went onto the driveway while I stayed on the stoop. I was busy keeping up with demand.

"Dad."

It was soft but emphatic.

I looked to my left to find my daughter, fresh out of snacks, braced against the garage door, penned there by three hungry deer. They had yet to grasp the concept of "all gone." They were each eager to relieve my harried daughter of the next offering which did not come. All we need do is yell and (or) make a sudden gesture; primal instinct does the rest. Neither of us had the presence of mind to do this. These were our guests. We didn't want to frighten them off. I slowly moved to the rescue and the situation was brought to a peaceful conclusion.

Duke will stand stock still and watch the proceedings with wide-eyed wonder. Quiche, however, must remain inside because she has inherited certain traits of her ancestry. Once, we left the door open just enough, and a brown bullet streaked out. The deer scattered to the four winds, and it took us several minutes to round up our recalcitrant pet.

No hard feelings, apparently. These "regulars" continue to come around mornings and late afternoons. They are always welcome.

www.ingramcontent.com/pod-product-compliance
Lightning Source LLC
Chambersburg PA
CBHW021333190726
48288CB00003B/1090

9781961254251